Escape from the French

Escape from the French

CAPTAIN HEWSON'S NARRATIVE
(1803–1809)

Edited and with an Introduction by Antony Brett-James

Hodder and Stoughton
in association with Webb & Bower

The publishers would like to thank Myra Thompson who has
made the publication of this book possible.

Published in Great Britain 1981 by
Webb & Bower (Publishers) Limited,
33 Southernhay East, Exeter, Devon EX1 1NS,
in association with Hodder and Stoughton Limited,
Mill Road, Dunton Green, Sevenoaks, Kent.

Designed by Malcolm Couch

Picture research by Anne-Marie Ehrlich

British Library Cataloguing in Publication Data

Hewson, Maurice
  Escape from the French.
  1. Europe — History — 1789–1815 — Personal
  narratives
  I. Title
  940.27'0924

ISBN 0–340–26240–0

Composition by Filmtype Services Limited,
Scarborough, England

Printed and bound in Great Britain by A. Wheaton & Co Ltd,
Exeter

Contents

Note modern spellings of Hewson's original place-names.

On the maps the place-names have been spelt strictly in accordance with Maurice Hewson's often erroneous transcriptions, rather than with the edited amendments in the text which are designed to help the reader identify the places more readily. Modern versions like Guingamp, Aigues-Mortes, Uzès, Rastatt and Biberach are more familiar.

Aigues-Mortes (Aiguwmorte), Ammer (River Amper), Bar-le-Duc (Bar le Duc), Biberach (Gibenbach), Camaret Fort (Camarét Fort), Chatillon (Chantillon), Chaumont en Bassigny (Chaumont in Bassine), Chiem (Lake of Kemere), Freiburg (im Bresgau) (Friburg), Guingamp (Guingeramp), Iller (River Iler), Kinzig (River Kinsin), Klagenfurt (Clagenfort), Landivisiau (Landeviseau), Lannion (Lanion), Mâcon (Maçon), Mont St Jean (Mont Sanjon), Memmingen (Meiningen), Nîmes (Nismes), Pont-à-Mousson (Ponto Mousson), Pont St Esprit (Pont d'Esprit), Rastatt (Radstadt), Rottweil (Rothweil), Saarlouis (Sarre-Louis), Saône (Soane), Schöngau (Shougan), Sète (Cette), Stes-Maries-de-la-Mer (St Maries), Tölz (Totz), Toul (Toule), Trévoux (Tréveux), Tuttlingen (Tutlingen), Uzès (Ures), Villach (Vilach), Weilheim (Welheim), Wertach (River Wardach).

Introduction

ACCOUNTS of attempts by prisoners of war to escape have always contained something of the attraction of high adventure with an individual, personal element as well. The odds are against the defenceless prisoner: fortress walls, armed sentries, daunting ramparts. Far from the line of battle, he also has to fight against despair of the soul, stagnation of the mind, deterioration of the body. In a backwater of war the drab monotony of life may break a man's spirit and sap his will to take action. It is natural that a majority of prisoners of war should settle down to getting through the monotony, to letting things slide, as month follows month. They resign themselves to the fact that only the end of hostilities will bring their release.

In the war against Napoleon the older prisoners of war, especially those of senior rank who no longer had any orders to give, became the most passive. The comparative few who refused to give way, who resented confinement and alien orders, who longed to be out and about, chafing as they did at being captive while great deeds were being done in the world outside, these were the escapers. For them prison presented a challenge; they simply had to escape. Most of them were young, fit and resilient. Out of over a hundred naval officers who made successful escapes, about ninety per cent were midshipmen. The more senior officers were on parole and refused to dishonour this by escaping. Moreover, they were likely, at least until 1806, to be exchanged, as happened in the case of Captains Brenton and Leveson-Gower. Junior officers on parole sought to have their parole rescinded by some misconduct so as to salve their consciences when about to escape. Prisoners held in Bitche under lock and key were not invited to give their parole, so they could not dishonour something which did not exist.

Even to scheme and plan kept a man sane and hopeful. Single-handed, or with two or three trusted companions, the crude means of escape would be collected: the rope made from bed linen or shirts; the nail, poker or file; the

PRODUITS DES DEUX MONDES

PH

L'ECHIQUI

le Passé.

le

l'A venir.

An anti-British caricature showing the French hope that the Order in Council dated 11 November 1807, by which the ports of France and her allies were to be blockaded by the British navy — in retaliation for Napoleon's Continental System — would end in ruin for Albion.

end of a boathook for use as a picklock or crampon. Two main problems inevitably faced the would-be escaper: getting out of the actual prison, and the journey across enemy country, and often hostile neighbouring states as well, until a friendly or neutral frontier was reached. But there were other problems; for instance, the real danger to life or limb if the home-made rope broke or proved too short and the escaper was dashed to pieces on the rocks far below. Then there was the risk of informers. At least two escape parties were betrayed to the French authorities by such people, and in another instance, when a Lieutenant Essel and fourteen fellow prisoners were all on a rope together, the rope was cut by an officer. Several were killed outright and not one escaped without a broken limb. However, despite every hazard, freedom, life, 'England, home and beauty' were the prizes of success. Death, though possible, was not the inevitable price of failure.

After 1806, with the failure of all attempts to negotiate exchange cartels (*see* note 12) of prisoners of war, those who dreamed about escape became more determined, more daring, seeing as they did no end to the war and to their captivity. The prime motive, obviously, of those who did break out was the hope of liberty — 'a long-wished-for haven'. Not to be goaded by *gendarmes*, confined in underground cells, weighed down by humiliating chains while on the march under escort; not to be worried about passports, frontiers, inquisitive strangers: that was what they longed for. The other great prospect was to return to the war, to their regiments or ships, to their profession as officers. Few were promoted while in a French prison, and it was galling to hear of contemporaries, even juniors, gaining glory and promotion, while they were confined and in a professional dead end. To have broken out and got safely away did enable a man like Maurice Hewson to write that, now at last 'we could look forward to advancement as others had done'.

Estimates vary as to the number who broke out and got away to England or to the Royal Navy without being recaptured. In 1812 the French Government published a list of 355 British prisoners of war who had been successful. Out of 656 naval officers who were held by the French, British sources indicate that 120 escaped and a further 11 were released or exchanged. Whereas it is known that 170,389 British prisoners of war were taken during World War I and that the equivalent figure for World War II is 192,319, it seems to be impossible to find an accurate total of British prisoners held in France between 1803 and 1814. Near the end of the war the Committee at Verdun that managed the relief funds had 16,000 names on its books, and on balance this figure is probably near the mark. For 1810 a total is given of 11,458 prisoners of war. Whatever the total, there was always a strong imbalance between French and British captives, given the fact that Britain held over 80,000 French prisoners, most of them soldiers. Because of this imbalance, Napoleon was never able to treat his British prisoners in the ruthless, often humiliating way he dealt with those from Spain and from defeated Prussia, Austria, and Russia.

The task of watching the enemy fleet and blockading the harbours of France was an exacting one for the Royal Navy, since ships and crews alike were exposed to the rigours of wave and weather driven in by Atlantic winds, to the hazards of being on a lee shore, and to sheer exhaustion. Some British ships of the Fleet were lost through running at night or in very thick weather, others by venturing into the North Sea too late in the year. A few were captured by privateers, and several were stranded under fire after chasing French ships ashore. It comes as no surprise that, despite the Royal Navy's high level of seamanship, daring sometimes took the place of caution, and that between 1803 and the end of 1808 at least 27 British warships foundered or were wrecked off the French coast. Indeed, throughout the French Revolutionary and Napoleonic Wars from 1793 to 1815 the Royal Navy lost 254 ships by shipwreck, 75 more foundered, and 15 were destroyed by fire or blown up to prevent capture. Hence the preponderance of naval prisoners: not until the Peninsular War did the trickle of soldiers really begin, although the loss of several transports on hostile shores led some troops into captivity before 1808.

British prisoners of war were sent to depots in a score of French towns, though many of the soldiers and sailors were held at Givet and Valenciennes. Those against whom serious complaints were laid, who were defiant and refractory, and who, above all, escaped and were recaptured, found themselves confined at Sedan, Sarrelibre or, worst of all, the aptly named Bitche. This immensely strong fortress built by Vauban in eastern Lorraine was a masterpiece of its kind, and held in certain respects the daunting reputation and particular cachet of World War II Colditz.

All naval officers were sent to Verdun, and here they lived alongside the other class of British people held by Napoleon, the so called *détenus*. These were men taken during the renewal of hostilities after the Peace of Amiens. Britain had formally declared war on 18 May 1803, although Napoleon accused the British of seizing two French ships before this declaration. It was a trumped-up charge, but he retaliated not only by seizing British ships, including a Dover-bound packet in Calais harbour, but also — and this was

11

virtually a new departure in time of war — by arresting and interning every male Briton between the ages of eighteen and sixty, whether service or civilian, who happened to be on French soil. Napoleon's excuse was that adult males were liable for service in the militia, so they might one day become belligerents, not least when his projected invasion of England took place. During the short-lived peace, the British after eight years of deprivation, had rushed across the Channel to visit France. Not only the rich and aristocratic had taken advantage of such a chance to travel again, though seventy peers and more than forty of their elder sons and other children had made the journey. Doctors, clergymen, artists, scholars, lawyers, engineers, businessmen and shopkeepers had also gone, in many cases with their families. So too had jockeys, servants, grooms, even members of the criminal class. Though some were warned in time to leave France before Napoleon's edict, the rest were detained while travelling on the faith of passports issued to them by the French Government. The majority of the five hundred or so *détenus* were kept at Verdun, where they lived on parole in private houses.

Drinking and smoking clubs were soon established. A gambling house flourished, where fortunes were lost to professional swindlers from Paris. On flat ground outside the town a race-course was laid out at great expense for summer meetings and, to quote one *détenu*, 'every midshipman was becoming a horseman, every sailor a groom, and everyone prided himself on his knowledge in horse flesh'. In short, 'Verdun offered in a small focus the spectacle of all the extravagance and dissipation of a capital, and might for noise and bustle be considered a little London.'*

Among the British naval officers imprisoned at Verdun and Bitche was Maurice Hewson, the author of *Escape from the French*. His family, who also called themselves Hewetson until at least the middle of the eighteenth century, were descended from a merchant who lived in York during the reigns of Henry VIII, Queen Mary and Queen Elizabeth. One of his sons, Thomas, living in Kildare, served as a Captain in King Charles I's Loyal Irish Protestant Army until it was disbanded by Cromwell in 1649. The Hewson family produced not a few members who made their mark, often as doctors, clergymen and scholars, but now and then in other fields of activity. There was, for instance, a sculptor who, from his studio in Rome, exhibited at the Royal Academy and whose masterpiece is a marble monument of a Provost of Trinity College, Dublin. Another example is

* Henry Lawrence *A Picture of Verdun* (1810) i, 90–91, 125.

Robert Hewetson who in 1794 commanded a contingent of Antiguans who volunteered to assist in the capture of the French West Indies. In later life he did take Holy Orders and was chaplain in HMS *Neptune* which fought at Trafalgar. And we have William Hewetson, born in 1786, who served with distinction in the Commissariat Department and who in 1846 chartered a ship to bring a cargo of Indian corn from America at his own expense to alleviate the terrible sufferings caused by the Irish potato famine. He declined the knighthood offered to him by a grateful Government.

Branches of the family had their base in Counties Limerick and Cork, but to reach Maurice Hewson we come by line of descent to John Hewson of Ennismore, Co. Kerry, who married in 1737 Margaret, the seventh daughter of Maurice Fitzgerald, Knight of Kerry. Tradition has it that while out riding over the very rough roads between Ennismore and Limerick, Miss Margaret Fitzgerald found that her horse had cast a shoe or gone lame. She and her groom were at a loss how to proceed when Mr John Hewson happened to come riding along the same road on a good horse, the loan of which he begged her to accept. He walked at her side to the house of her friends, and this chance acquaintance led to their betrothal. At the time of his marriage John Hewson leased from his father-in-law the 1,170 acres of the Ennismore estate.

The eldest son of this marriage was Francis, in 1758 a scholar of Trinity College, Dublin, who became Archdeacon of Aghadoe near Killarney. While he was still Rector of Kilgobbin in September 1773 he married Margaret Sandes of Kilcavan, Queen's County, who bore him seven sons and a daughter, who was also called Margaret. The eldest boy was John Francis of Ennismore. Next came George Francis (1776–1860), who joined the Royal Navy at the age of twelve and was fortunate enough to serve in two ships under the command of Thomas Foley, one of Nelson's best Captains. At the attack against the French in Toulon in 1794, commanded at sea by Admiral Lord Hood, Midshipman George Hewson led a party of seamen in the fighting on shore. (It was at Toulon also that Napoleon Bonaparte first attracted the high esteem of his superiors while serving as a young Lieutenant-Colonel of artillery.) In the following year George was promoted Lieutenant, having passed his examination in front of Nelson in person.

Of the remaining sons born to the Rev. Francis and Margaret Hewson, there followed Francis David, Robert, Lancelot, and Thomas, who in 1819 became President of the Royal College of Surgeons, Ireland. The seventh and youngest was Maurice, born on 5 November 1786. At an early age he decided to follow his brother George into the Royal Navy. This he did without benefit of his father's counsel, for Archdeacon Francis Hewson died at Woodford, Co. Kerry, on 15 August 1789 — a month after the storming of the Bastille and the start of one of the most momentous and eventful quarter-centuries in the history of Europe.

Maurice Hewson began his service in the Royal Navy on 21 May 1796 as an Able Seaman in the sloop *Savage* (16 guns), commanded by Captain George Winchworth. At the end of the year he was transferred to HMS *Overyssel* (64 guns), flagship of Admiral Peyton, and served in her until June 1797, the last three months as a Midshipman. Most of this service was in the Downs, that comparatively safe anchorage between the North and South Foreland in Kent, sheltered by the Goodwin Sands. As a result of attending a sick messmate, Hewson contracted a fever and was sent, as he tells us, 'to sick quarters, but Mrs Capn. Winchworth had me moved to her home till it pleased God to restore me to health'. He was invalided at Deal Hospital, where the doctors advised him to stay on shore until he had fully recovered his health. Deciding to spend the time at home in Ireland, he took passage from the Downs in a merchant ship and immediately ran into trouble.

> I was taken prisoner to Calais by a Row Boat which captured the Sloop out of Dover Roads. Thro' the generous interference of the Prussian Consul who claimed me as a relative and read my naval certificates which were found on me as discharges from a bricklayer; and sending to me his son's coat to dress in he succeeded in getting my release and after a very short detention I reappeared among my friends.

Hewson remained at home through the winter of 1797–8, but in March, thanks to the intervention of his brother George, Captain Robert Dudley Oliver took him in HMS *Nemesis* (28 guns). As soon as fitted for sea, *Nemesis* escorted a convoy across the Atlantic to Quebec and on her return was stationed in the Downs as part of a squadron observing the movement of French ships off Calais and Boulogne. When Captain Oliver was transferred to command HMS *Mermaid* (32 guns) he was pleased to take Hewson with him. To begin with, their station was off Brest under Lord Bridport's command, but when part of the French fleet managed to slip away to the Mediterranean, *Mermaid* was sent with a squadron of ten sail of the line to reinforce Admiral Lord Keith there.

Maurice Hewson relates that in the space of thirteen months 'the Boat

Admiralty Office, 26 Feb. 1803

Gentlemen,

WHEREAS the Bearer hereof, *Mr. Maurice Hewson* has made Application to the Lords Commiſſioners of the Admiralty that he may be examined touching his Qualifications to perform the Duty of a Lieutenant in His Majeſty's Navy; I am commanded by their Lordſhips to ſignify their Directions to you, to proceed to examine him accordingly; and in caſe it ſhall appear to you that he has ſerved Six Years at Sea, and has been rated Two of the ſaid Six Years as Midſhipman, or Mate, in ſome of His Majeſty's Ships; and that he does produce regular Journals, and good Certificates from the Commanders he has ſerved with, of his Sobriety, Diligence, and Qualifications of an Able Seaman; and that upon your own Examination, you find he has attained to a ſufficient Knowledge, both in the Practick Part and Theory of Navigation, and you ſhall be ſatisfied that he is not under Twenty Years of Age, you are then to give him a Certificate, expreſſing therein his particular Qualifications.

2 March 1803 I am,

J. S. H. Pitt

D. McWainwright

               Gentlemen,

Your moſt humble Servant,

Wm. Marsden

A letter from the Admiralty Office instructing that Maurice Hewson be examined for promotion to Lieutenant. In March 1803 his age was sixteen and a half, yet he was supposed to be 'not under Twenty Years of Age'. In the accompanying list of ships detailing the length of time he served in each, Hewson is shown as having been seventeen, not ten, when he entered the Royal Navy in 1796 and twenty-two in 1803. Perhaps the discrepancy was deliberate.

cutt out from under the Batteries 72 vessels many of which were hard contested actions and much gallantry and individual bravery was conspicuous.' *Mermaid* cruised in the Mediterranean until after the defeat of Bonaparte's army in Egypt and the signing of the Peace of Amiens in 1802. Then, in Hewson's account of what happened, 'We were ordered to attend Lord Hutchinson who returned from the Command of the Troops in Egypt much fatigued and in delicate health whom we conveyed with his brother [Christopher Hely-Hutchinson] to several places in Sicily and Naples where the Commander of the Expedition to Egypt was treated with distinguished honor and hospitality.'

On her return to England *Mermaid* was paid off. Fortunately for Hewson, every effort was made to retain him on the much reduced peace establishment, and he was appointed to the 28-gun frigate, HMS *Diamond* (Captain Thomas Elphinstone), 'then proceeding with the Dutch Troops to the Texel where not being acquainted with the passage grounded on the sands at the entrance where we remained till weather moderated when we succeeded after lightening the Ship to get her off and safe into the Texel.'

Back in Portsmouth, *Diamond* in her turn was paid off, recommissioned and docked. 'Shortly after I passed my examination for a Lieutenant [25 February 1803], which the passing Commissioners were pleased to say reflected much credit on me and wrote to Captn Elphinstone to that effect and recommending me for promotion.' But Hewson was not to be promoted for a further six years, thanks to his falling into the hands of the French soon after hostilities were resumed.

The next five years are covered by Hewson's narrative. Captured on shore outside Brest during the night of 4–5 September 1803, Midshipman Hewson eventually reached the fortress of Verdun in eastern France on 14 January 1804. From this long period of confinement one letter to his mother survives. It bears the date 'June 16th 1805 at Verdun sur Meuse'. After lamenting her recent and dangerous illness, and giving news that his brother George had been appointed to *Royal Sovereign* — Admiral Collingwood's flagship at Trafalgar — Maurice writes of arrangements by which money can be sent to him in France through George's Navy Agents in London and a firm of bankers in Lombard Street. His letter goes on:

I cannot my dearest Mother console you as yet with any prospects of an exchange but assure you I pass my time as agreable as it is possible when that I am tired of reading or writing which I am very fond of were not my eyes so very weak. I step down and join in society with my old Land Lady

Rear-Admiral Cuthbert Collingwood (1750–1810), from a mezzotint by Henry Howard (1796–1847) dating from *c.* 1802. Collingwood was created a baron after Trafalgar, where he was Nelson's Second-in-Command.

and her daughter whose conversation I not only find extremely agreable but every way instructive.

On 21 October that same year George Hewson fought at the battle of Trafalgar as acting First Lieutenant in HMS *Dreadnought*, to which he had recently moved from *Royal Sovereign*. More than two years were to elapse before Maurice made his first bid for freedom. For this daring venture his companion was a fellow Midshipman named Butterfield, of HMS *Impétueux*, who had come to Verdun in the previous May. Together they broke out on 13 March 1808, and a month later had reached the south of France and Aigues-Mortes. Here good fortune deserted them and they were obliged to give themselves up. In chains the two escaped prisoners of war were escorted to the dreaded fortress of Bitche, known to many as 'the Mansion of Tears'. They reached it on the second day of August.

To most prisoners this would have been a major set-back, even a permanent one. Hewson was not deterred. Barely six weeks after entering Bitche he made his escape, this time under the experienced leadership of a former shipmate, Donat Henchy O'Brien, for whom the breakout on 15 September 1808 was to be the fourth attempt, though only the first from Bitche itself. With two companions, one of whom had to be left behind in Germany because of illness, they crossed the Rhine and made their way through Baden, Württemberg and Bavaria with many an anxious moment until they reached Austria and a comparatively friendly welcome. On arrival at the port of Trieste they were able to rejoin the Royal Navy, thanks to the presence of two frigates cruising nearby.

At the end of his narrative Maurice Hewson finds himself serving in HMS *Magnificent* (74 guns), with his rank of Lieutenant confirmed by the Admiralty on 15 July 1809. He and O'Brien, who was now in *Warrior*, wrote the first draft of their escape stories at the request of the Governor of Malta, Sir Alexander Ball, who with his usual generosity of spirit proposed to forward the accounts to the Admiralty in support of his recommendations for their promotion. While on board *Magnificent*, Hewson says: 'During my vacant moments I was occupied writing this unvarnished tale of facts.' On his return to Malta he was sad to learn that Ball had just died.

Whereas Hewson's account now appears for the first time more than 170 years after the events and excitements he describes, O'Brien's story was published in *The Naval Chronicle* and then in book form in 1814 under the title *My Adventures during the Late War*, with an enlarged edition in two volumes coming from the press twenty-five years later. The full title was *My*

INTRODUCTION

Adventures during the Late War: comprising a Narrative of Shipwreck, Captivity, Escapes from French prisons, etc from 1804 to 1827.

Maurice Hewson emerges from his narrative as an officer who, despite his youth, looked after his fellow prisoners on the march and in cells after first being captured, and who set them a good example. Rather than idle his time away in gambling at Verdun, he occupied himself in the study of French and Italian, and later of German. Throughout his ordeal he derived strong comfort from the Protestant faith, and time and again he writes about committing himself 'to the care of Him who looks down on all his creatures' and looking 'to the Lord as a friend that never faileth those who call upon Him in the hour of need'. In times of stress, danger and acute disappointment he turns to God's protection; when things go smoothly, when obstacles are overcome and perils avoided, Hewson never forgets to thank God for His many blessings and mercies.

Hewson was astonished by the high spirits he and Butterfield enjoyed while escaping, 'every difficulty or disentanglement only giving cause to joke on the occasion'. To discover in themselves resourcefulness, ingenuity under interrogation, boldness, cool judgement, *sang froid* and the other qualities required by prisoners of war on the run served to deepen their already considerable experience and maturity of spirit. 'We had many hair-breadth escapes of being arrested', Hewson admits, 'which inspired us with confidence and a presence of mind which the occasion demanded.' Even failure was considered a preparation for future undertakings.

After his final escape and soon after joining HMS *Magnificent*, Maurice Hewson had an opportunity of earning his Captain's trust and esteem. It so happened that Captain George Eyre was a stranger to Valetta Harbour, by now well known to Hewson, and when a violent gale blew up while the ship was cruising off Malta, he entrusted Hewson with the duty of navigating her into harbour. This he did with skill and good seamanship. By this time Maurice had learnt that his brother George, having taken part in the 1807 expedition to Copenhagen, had recently been promoted to the rank of Commander — in fact, on the very same date as his own promotion had been confirmed — and was involved that summer of 1809 in the sorry operations against the island of Walcheren at the mouth of the Scheldt.

The Mediterranean Fleet in which both Hewson and O'Brien were now serving had the tasks of protecting British maritime communications, cutting those of the enemy, and preventing French warships, particularly those at Toulon, from executing some sudden *coup*. The moment Napoleon thrust into southern Italy, and once he had moved in the direction of the

19

The town and Old Fort of Corfu. Corfu and Paxo were the only two
Ionian Islands not captured from the French by the British in the
expedition of 1809 and 1810, in which Maurice Hewson played a
prominent part. The drawing, by John Davy, comes from his *Notes
and Observations on the Ionian Islands and Malta* (1842).

Balkans and Turkey, control of the Adriatic became even more vital to British interests. By the terms of the Treaty of Tilsit France gained the Ionian Islands, and their seizure by enemy troops posed a threat alike to northern Greece and to Collingwood's position. Although always short of ships with which to carry out taxing and overstretched responsibilities, this patient, persevering and determined Admiral increased his strength in the Adriatic, mainly under Captain Hoste's energetic command. But he also urged the military commanders to action. Surely with naval support some at least of these islands could be wrested from their garrisons. Moreover, a port in British hands at the entrance to the Adriatic was highly to be desired.

Accordingly, in October 1809, a force of some 1,800 men commanded by Brigadier-General John Oswald went with HMS *Magnificent* and *Warrior* and other ships to the island of Zante. Here the small Italian garrison surrendered. Cephalonia gave in next without resistance. Detachments then landed unopposed on Ithaca and Cerigo, the latter island surrendering to Hewson's fellow prisoner during his first two years at Verdun, namely Captain Jahleel Brenton, now in command of HMS *Spartan*. The winter passed, and on 21 March 1810 an expedition, comprising *Magnificent*, a frigate, a brig-sloop, three gun-boats and five transports, having on board about 1,800 troops under Oswald's command, sailed from Zante and arrived off the mountainous island of Santa Maura (now Levkas). The soldiers, reinforced by marines and by 150 seamen from *Magnificent* under Maurice Hewson, together with ten of her 18-pounders, in spite of some slight opposition managed to land. On 16 April, after hard fighting and an eight-day bombardment, the French garrison defending the fortress of Amaxichi in the north-east corner of the island surrendered. Only a few hours before this final event, Captain Eyre, who had been wounded while on shore, found himself so short of officers in *Magnificent* that he recalled Hewson on board, thereby depriving his Lieutenant of a mention in the Gazette which announced the occupation of Santa Maura. Of the Ionian Islands, only Corfu remained in French hands, and its garrison of 4,000 men was too strong to attack with the forces available, so the navy maintained a blockade instead.

Hewson continued to serve in HMS *Magnificent* until February 1812. Four months went by before he joined his next ship, *Clarence* (74 guns), in the Channel. Whether he had a chance of visiting Ireland is not known, but on 2 July, the day after he went on board *Clarence*, his mother, Margaret Hewson, died in Limerick at the age of seventy-two.

While in HMS *Clarence* Hewson once again had opportunities of showing his courage, coolness in action, initiative and good leadership. On one particular occasion, while in command of the boats during an action with a strong force of French gun-vessels, he displayed such high gallantry and seamanship that on his return to his own ship the Captain, Henry Vansittart, presented him on the quarter-deck with the very sword which he himself had been given on first going to sea. Such was his regard for Maurice Hewson.

He continued to serve in *Clarence* until 28 June 1814, by which time Napoleon had abdicated and gone into exile on Elba: and during this period Hewson was frequently sent ashore with flags of truce in order to test the loyalty of the French authorities and to induce them to join the Bourbon standard of King Louis XVIII. Thanks to his years as a prisoner of war he had a considerable command of the French language, and he had the satisfaction of seeing his efforts of persuasion crowned with complete and flattering success.

In March 1815 Napoleon escaped from Elba, landed in southern France, and returned in triumph to Paris. Two months later Hewson was appointed First Lieutenant to the sloop *Prometheus* (16 guns), again in the English Channel. Napoleon, after his defeat on the field of Waterloo and his failure to rally support in Paris for yet another campaign, was thought to be trying to escape to North America and HMS *Prometheus* was part of one naval force charged with intercepting the vanquished Emperor off Ushant, while other ships cruised expectantly off La Rochelle and Rochefort, off Cape Finisterre and in the Channel. On 15 July Napoleon surrendered to Captain Maitland on board HMS *Bellerophon*, and Hewson's ship, commanded by Captain William Bateman Dashwood, was one of the escort into Tor Bay near Plymouth. *Prometheus* proved to be Maurice Hewson's last ship. He left her in September that year.

In May 1816 Maurice's brother George obtained post rank as Captain, but ill health obliged him to retire from the navy soon afterwards. Thirty-five years later he was promoted on seniority to Rear-Admiral.

During his exile on the island of St Helena, Napoleon said of the British Navy: 'Wherever there is water to float a ship, we are sure to find you in the way.' In fact, the first years of the nineteenth century, up to Napoleon's death in 1821, were a period of intensive and revolutionary development in the propulsion of ships. Thanks to James Watts's double engine, patented in 1781, and Patrick Miller's paddle wheels six years later, the path was open for the harnessing of steam power to ships. In 1802 the paddle tug

History of Services,
&c.
(continued.)

The Work being in a state of forwardness, it is EARNESTLY solicited, to ensure accuracy in the Memoirs, that this Formula
BE FILLED UP AND RETURNED, WITH AS LITTLE DELAY AS POSSIBLE, addressed to WILLIAM R. O'BYRNE, ESQ.,
9, DOUGHTY STREET, RUSSELL SQUARE, LONDON.

Those desirous of possessing a copy of the Work are requested to signify their wish to the Author.

Facsimile of Maurice Hewson's handwritten account of part of his early naval service, prepared in 1845 for the *Naval Biographical Dictionary* by William O'Byrne (1823–96), published in 1849.

Charlotte Dundas towed barges along Scottish canals, to the alarm of canal owners who feared damage to the banks. Arthur Woolf's double-cylinder expansion engine dates from 1804, and in 1812 the *Comet* began to steam from Glasgow to Greenock three times a week. The year of Waterloo saw a paddle steamer make the journey from Greenock to London. And in 1819 the full-rigged sailing ship *Savannah*, aided by an auxiliary steam engine, crossed the Atlantic from her namesake port in Georgia to Liverpool in twenty-seven days. By 1821 steamboats were crossing between Dover and Calais, and in that same year the Royal Navy introduced its first steam tug, the *Monkey*.

Naval officers had long had to contend with the threat of a ship being becalmed at a crucial moment, and it was no less intensely frustrating to be pinned inside a harbour waiting for a favourable wind to get out to the open sea. Even so, a tug could originally only tow a Royal Navy ship of the line out of confined waters and no further concessions to steam were countenanced for a decade. The Admiralty actively discouraged the use of steam vessels, because in their view they were 'calculated to strike a fatal blow at the naval supremacy of the Empire'. This did not prevent men of vision like Lord Cochrane from agitating for steam power to be used in ships of war.

Although precise evidence has proved difficult to find, it is clear that, judging by the account of his service penned by Maurice Hewson for William O'Byrne's *Naval Biographical Dictionary*, he was closely involved with these developments in steam. Indeed, O'Byrne claims that Hewson was 'the very first person who established the practicability of a double-engine to the purposes of steam navigation, as he was also to navigate a steam vessel on the Atlantic'.

In 1830 Maurice Hewson was living on the southern shores of the Shannon estuary at Loghill, Co. Limerick, the home of his brother Francis David. That July he married Anna, the daughter of a Dublin barrister-at-law named John Hunt. Her family home was in Upper Merrion Street. Of the three children born to them, the only son Francis emigrated to New Zealand and worked in the Public Works Department until his retirement in 1907, when he lived in Thames Valley, Auckland. One of his daughters, Annie, married a New Zealander called Innis and bore nine girls and seven boys. Two of Francis Hewson's sons went to America: Frank worked in California as engineer to a water supply company, while by 1907 Harry was assistant engineer to a company building a railroad in Oregon.

The marriage of Maurice and Anna Hewson lasted for almost forty years, and during this period they moved house frequently. Records are scant for the first decade, but the year 1844 finds them at Claremorris, Co. Mayo. Six years later the Dublin Directory shows their home as Rathgar Lodge in Upper Rathmines, and by 1853 they were living in the village of Roundtown at Fortfield Lodge on Terenure Road, Dublin, and they stayed there until 1860. It was from this house that their younger daughter, Maria Margaret, was married, in 1858, to Edmund Davy of Kimmage Lodge, Terenure. He was the son of a professor of chemistry of the same name who worked at the Royal Cork Institution and then at the Royal Dublin Society. Edmund Davy's first cousin was the brilliant scientist Sir Humphry Davy (1778–1829), discoverer of laughing gas and inventor of the safety lamp for miners.

The Hewsons' next move took them to 4A, Kenilworth Square East in Rathgar, but within two years their address was Mount Prospect on the Upper Rathgar Road. Here they remained until 1866. Subsequent records show that on and off they shared the Hunt family house, number 10, Upper Merrion Street, Dublin, with a Mrs Hunt, who was presumably the widow of one of Anna Hewson's brothers. Certainly all these moves suggest not only that Captain Hewson — his rank sometimes appears as Commander and sometimes as Captain, by courtesy — was a restless man but also that he was renting rather than buying premises (a usual practice in Victorian Dublin).*

Captain Hewson died of chronic bronchitis at 10, Upper Merrion Street, Dublin, on 30 December 1869. In his will, dated 31 January 1867, Hewson left effects worth not more than £1,500. He bequeathed to his wife Anna

> ... all my household furniture plate and farming utensils Horses and Carriages. Being possessed of Twenty shares in the Provincial Bank I give and bequeath unto my dear wife Anna the dividends and annual produce of twelve of said shares (which I intend for my son Francis) for and during the term of her natural life.

His unmarried daughter, Annie Elizabeth Lombard, was to receive the

---

* I am greatly indebted to Miss Rosemary ffolliott for her excellent and persevering researches in Dublin into the Hewson family and the constant moves of Maurice and his wife.

dividends and annual produce of the remaining eight shares during his wife's lifetime and as long as she continued to reside with her mother. Thereafter the eight shares would go to his married daughter, Maria Margaret Davy.

In a codicil he transferred to Maria Margaret the eight shares in the Provincial Bank. Less than a month after signature of the will, his spinster daughter Annie married Robert Adamson of Lisgarriff House, Lecarrow, near Loughrea, Co. Roscommon.

Mrs Hewson survived her husband Maurice by barely two years, and died at Lisgarriff House on 22 January 1872, at the age of eighty-one. The Adamsons had two daughters, but as neither girl married, their line died out. In contrast, Maria Margaret Davy bore six children. One of her granddaughters married a Mr Stanley C. L. Thompson, and through him Captain Maurice Hewson's narrative of his escape from the French passed to the present owner, Mrs Myra Thompson, when she inherited the manuscript.

Escape from the French

CAPTAIN HEWSON'S NARRATIVE
(1803–1809)

If Time's uncouth and jarring phrases wound
The softer sense with inharmonious sound,
Yet let her list'ning sympathy prevail
While conscious truth unfolds her piteous tale.

Multum ille et terris jactatus et alto
Multo quoque et bello passus.

Virg. Aen. Lib. 1.[1]

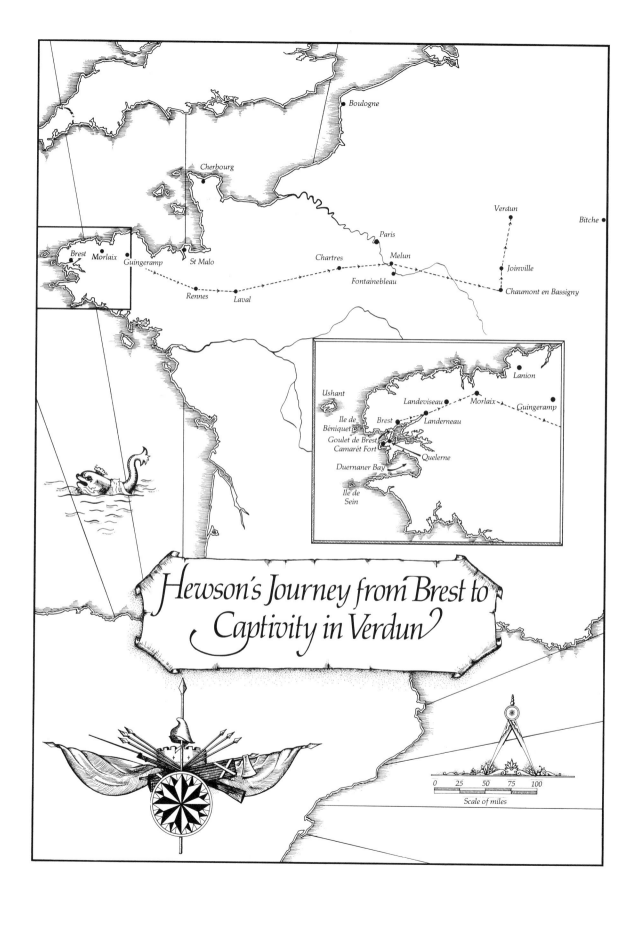

Boulogne

Cherbourg

Verdun

Bitche

Paris

Brest
Morlaix
Guingeramp
St Malo

Chartres

Melun

Joinville

Rennes
Laval

Fontainebleau

Chaumont en Bassigny

Lanion

Ushant

Landeviseau
Morlaix
Guingeramp

Ile de
Béniquet
Brest
Landerneau

Goulet de Brest
Camarét Fort
Quelerne

Duernaner Bay

Ile de
Sein

Hewson's Journey from Brest to Captivity in Verdun

0   25   50   75   100

Scale of miles

I

Capture

AT the recommencement of the war in 1803[2] being then attached to the *Diamond*, proceeding from Portsmouth in the month of July to join the Channel Fleet, when off Weymouth, we detained a Dutch Ship in which Captain [Thomas] Elphinstone despatched me as Prize Master. When I had safely given up my charge to the Agents at Portsmouth, not finding a man-of-war likely to sail for some time to the Westward, the Admiral was good enough to allow me to go in a passage vessel to Plymouth, and on the evening of my arriving there, was so fortunate as to get into the *Pickle*, just about getting under weigh for the Channel Fleet. At arriving off Brest, to my disappointment, the *Diamond* had departed on a cruise to the westward, and until an opportunity might offer of sending me to join her, the Admiral directed me to remain in the Schooner. Mr. [John Richards] Lapenotiere, the Commander, very frequently entrusted me with command of his boats in attacks on small vessels coasting along shore. I generally succeeded in bringing them off to the schooner, and was so fortunate as to attract the notice of Admiral Collingwood[3] who was pleased to say that he would take the first opportunity to recommend me to the Admiralty.

On the evening of the 4th of September, the Admiral sent an order to direct that the boats should be given to me to endeavour to procure for him some small boat coming out of Brest, to ascertain from her crew if a report prevailed of a counter-revolution said to have arisen in Paris by some passengers, which they told the Admiral was headed by Morreau.[4] The entrance, or Gûllet [le Goulet], going into Brest is strongly protected by batteries and fortifications on each side. The Ship Battery is the most prominent on the right hand shore: from thence are a succession of smaller ones as far as Camaret Fort to prevent our ships from approaching sufficiently near to reconnoitre their ships in Brest. When dark I left the schooner, and at about 11 o'clock landed on a rock which projected from the shore within reach of gunshot of the Ship Battery. When I had placed keepers in the boat and arranged all ready for an instant shove-off from the shore, and men on different points to look out, I took one man with me to the summit of the rock to see if we had been observed by the sentinels from a small Fort which was immediately over us. Seeing all quiet, I was in the act of again returning to the boat, when from an overlooking projection I was much surprised to see the boat pulling away, when, regardless of giving alarm, I hailed them to return, but to no effect. Hurrying down I was met by those whom I had stationed at the different points in consternation at the keepers running away with the boat.

Seeing our capture inevitable, I endeavoured to reconcile the crew to their fate, for British seamen have a great dread of the severities of imprisonment. I proposed to them getting into the interior with me and endeavouring our escape thro' one of the fishing boats in Douarnenez Bay, but to this it was objected, that if discovered, we should be treated as spies. At daybreak seeing our schooner not more than three miles from us, and a strong ebb tide, I proposed swimming to her, and at all risks returning with a boat to take them off, if permitted — but this equally alarmed them (being left without me). As the day advanced some vessels came to anchor at a short distance from where I was concealed, the which had my boat been left me would have been my prizes. I shewed myself from the rock to them, and put on me the appearance of a deserter, to induce them to send a boat to me with the intent of seizing on them had I led them to come to me. About seven o'clock our own Boat, manned with Frenchmen and one of the deserters, came to look for us. At first they seemed timid, and wanted me to swim off (not wishing to approach the shore). The soldiers, of which there was a party, cocked their pieces at me to oblige me to do so, but with seeming indifference I turned round to walk up to the Fort to surrender myself, and to my astonishment saw soldiers like bees surrounding me on every side.

After a little *parler* they took us in the boat to Camaret Fort, where Mons. le Commandant honoured us with a salute of three volleys. We were the first led captive to his Fort this war. When they had searched us scrupulously for papers they sent us to the yard where we found the deserters, Michael Connors and Michael Owens. 'Twas now for the first time that I felt the indignity of being exposed to the malevolence of two lost unhappy men, actuated by every various passion of desperation — at one moment breathing vengeance against their King, their country, their parents, and against the fancied tyranny of their officers — the next moment reciprocally accusing each other of their rash deed, and then fawning to the men for forgiveness, whom I desired as they valued their

Country, or my little protection, not to be seen even to speak to them, which was strictly observed, but answered on the part of the deserters by a little abuse, and the comfortable prospect of 'each being officers in their turn'; a reward they sanguinely looked to for their deed. About nine o'clock we left Fort Camaret under an escort for the main guard at Quelerne, which was nearly four miles distant. A gentleman who told me he was Swedish Consul at Brest came as interpreter and by him we were separately interrogated as to our capture: I was the last examined and by the questions proposed to me I had every reason to believe that every means was tried to extort from the men the sentiments of the seamen serving in the Fleet — whether any armament of troops were embarked etc. The remainder of the day I passed walking about with the officers without any apparent restraint — the men being with the soldiers in the Barracks.

While sitting in the officers' mess-room (which looked to me more a thoroughfare for all, 'Hail, fellows, well met' — officers and men seemed equally to act without *embarras* and a familiarity inconsistent with discipline) Michael Owens came to request a drink of water, and was ordered a tumbler of wine. He muttered some sorrow at its falling to my lot to command the boat, but that his desertion had been an act previously determined with Connors. He was sure that he should be rewarded, and after inveighing in his former strain at the severity and tyranny of our service drank off 'Damnation to the British Constitution.'

The Interpreter was extremely attentive to me, but through a tone of insinuation which he was practising, I saw his chief object was to draw from me every possible information of the state of England. He told me of the partiality of his wife and daughters for the English, and that the latter were learning our language — then would intimate a surprise that we would not meditate an attack on Brest, which could be sustained a sufficient time to allow us to destroy the Fleet and Arsenal. Thus he tried various means to discover our force and the general feeling of England on the subject of the war — to all which I answered with seeming indifference.

I passed this day in a kind of stupor, tormented by repeated questions and reflections: at length supper came in to my relief, after which they showed me the busts of Buonaparte and W. Pitt[5] — the latter was miserably reviled, as being the cause of many evils to France. They told me that they were determined to extirpate him as their only remaining enemy, for they 'should soon be in England'. They asked me if I had any sisters to whom I would recommend them, and talked of the manner in which they would treat my fair friends before long. Many similarly low illiberal jests ended by

Brest naval base, c. 1823. It shows the Castle, part of the Arsenal, and the River Penfeld.
This is one of a series of sixty-four 'Views of the Principal Ports of France', painted by the
distinguished marine artist, Louis Garneray (1783–1857).

the breaking of the bust of W. Pitt. I was sent to a room to sleep with the Sergeants and Corporals, but being as ill pleased with this part of their treatment of me as the former, begged to be imprisoned with my men, where a wisp of straw formed my pillow — weariness, the rest.

The following afternoon we were conducted in a small boat to Brest, passing through the Fleet in the roadstead, and were delivered over to the main Guard. The General sent me a supper, & some wine, and the officer was civil to me. The next day Septr. the 7th I was conducted before the Municipality where I underwent a *procès-verbal*[6], and thence to a prison in the Arsenal on the opposite side of the creek from the town, where we were all confined to separate rooms. That which was given me to locate was clean and had open air. My bed was straw, and my subsistence a pound and half of brown bread and calavanse[7] soup at noon. All communication with the men was denied me.

When I had been a few days in this confinement I wrote to the Commandant at Brest to explain the different conduct held to prisoners in England. After stating the allowance given them, I demanded that protection due by him to us as prisoners of war, with the request to be allowed to visit my men at least once each day. To this I received no answer, but two days after (Septr. 15th.) two *Gens d'armes* [gendarmes] led me to Brest before two general Officers, and an Admiral, who enquired very minutely into the particulars of my being taken, and the purport of my coming on shore. They were conciliatory and distinct in their interrogation, but indeed asked me some questions which I did not feel myself at liberty to answer. When ended they offered me the *procès-verbal* for my signature, and were not pleased at my refusal, as suspecting them of writing more than I had truly stated; which I endeavoured to soften, by assuring them, through the interpreter, that I bore them every respect, as the officers of a nation particularly distinguished for its humanity to prisoners of war, but I was assured what they felt for their own country were they in my situation would dictate to them the impropriety of attaching their names to any public document. They then told me that they were thus particular for my sake; the deserters had asserted that I landed with a view of taking a plan of the Fortifications: and one went so far as to say that I was a Frenchman, and intended the succeeding night of my capture endeavouring to get into Brest. They were generous enough to tell me that they prevaricated in their evidence, which caused the greater part to be treated with contempt, but advised me to be prepared for a Court Martial as well as the remainder of my crew, who the deserters said were distinguished officers in disguise. The men were equally examined, who all asserted the cause of my coming to the rock to be, that I might the better conceal the Boat from view, to try and get a Fishing Boat with some fish for the Admiral.

I again wrote to the general commanding at Brest from my former room in the Arsenal to which I was reconducted protesting against the evidence of two men given in despair with a view to do away with any future accusation of their own guilt — that whatever form of trial he might be pleased to direct, I was confident its members would show every justice to unprotected individuals, and for myself it caused me no thought, but that I was much concerned that the seamen in the boat with me should be implicated, as they only obeyed their duty in pulling me to the station which I had been directed to take for the night, and the consequence of their disobedience would be merited punishment. For them I most earnestly entreated his humanity and felt assured that his own high sense of honor would not enforce their trial: *au reste*, we were taken in arms, and bearing the flag and uniform of our country.

On Sunday the 18th a *gen d'armes* came to liberate us from our confinement in the Arsenal, and conduct us to the Naval Hospital at Brest: this was a great relief to me and the men, though we met with humane and attentive treatment from the gaolkeeper — yet the change of diet to only hard brown bread with a basin of calavanse soup at noon was beginning to affect my health — for never believing it possible that it would fall to my lot to be made a prisoner in my turn in any of my excursions, I had not one shilling in my pocket, and had on me but a round jacket (luckily I had a great coat in the Boat) and therefore had nothing for support, but the prison allowance. No person ever came to see me but my gaoler with my bread and soup. The activity in the yard, and seeing a few ship-wrights at work at a Three-Decker (The *Bucentaure*[8]) which was building immediately under my window, and the convicts passing and repassing locked to each other with heavy chains, carrying heavy spars, served to beguile the time.

The Arsenal at Brest is built on low ground, quayed in from a narrow inlet, on both sides of a creek, and is very conveniently adapted for an Arsenal for Men-of-War, the water being so deep that the ships lie at the quays at each side. There were two 74-gun ships on the stocks: and the scene around seemed in the highest state of activity. The town of Brest is situated on a height having its old mouldering walls overhanging the Arsenal on its south side. We passed through a good deal of the town going to the Hospital, where I became a room-mate with a French Midshipman, who spoke a few words of English. Our meals were served to us in a clean comfortable manner, and a degree of deference and respect was now shewn me to which I had previously been a stranger. The Deserters were brought to the same Hospital, and were treated as my men. As I enjoyed free liberty to walk through the wards of the upper floor, I now saw my men regularly attended to and the kindest treatment shewn them.

At the time that the Convents were abolished in France in the year 1793, the Nuns were permitted to become Attendants to the Hospitals. They brought with them all their purity of manners and tenderness of disposition, speaking comfort even to the enemies of their country. A Miss Burke was *première Soeur* and in her benevolent and aimiable tenderness shewed that natural characteristic in which her country-women stand so pre-eminently high. By every little attention and kindness she tried to soften as much as in her lay the sorrow which she believed my captivity caused in my mind. This lady was of an Irish family — had been educated by them in France, and being left an orphan retired to a Convent: and though far stricken in years, love for her country was dearest to her heart. Each ward had its particular *soeur*: the lady attending us was a very kind woman: she procured me a change of linen and had my *only* shirt washed for me, and set all her friends at work to knit me stockings. The week that I spent at this Hospital was but to prepare me for the severity of the treatment that awaited me.

The Commandant very civilly sent his Secretary to make known to me that our march was ordered for Fontainebleau, and to proffer me in his name any necessaries of clothing that I should require. I requested for myself and each of my men a pair of trousers and stockings, and a shirt, giving just a change to preserve cleanliness on our route: money was proffered me, but as my Bill would not be accepted in return, I declined taking any.

Thus equipped on Sunday the 27th an escort came for us, and I bid a

Above: 'A Nautical Survey of the Bay of Brest and the Ushant Islands', dated 1807. This shows the Goulet, Camaret, Hodierne (Audierne), Douarnenez Bay and other places mentioned by Hewson. Captain Thomas Hurd RN (1757?–1823) also made the first exact survey of Bermuda and was hydrographer to the Admiralty from 1808 until his death.

Below: *Bucentaure*, on which shipwrights were working outside Hewson's window while he was held in Brest Arsenal during September 1803, mounted 80 guns. Two years later, at the battle of Trafalgar on 21 October 1805, *Bucentaure* was Admiral Villeneuve's flagship.

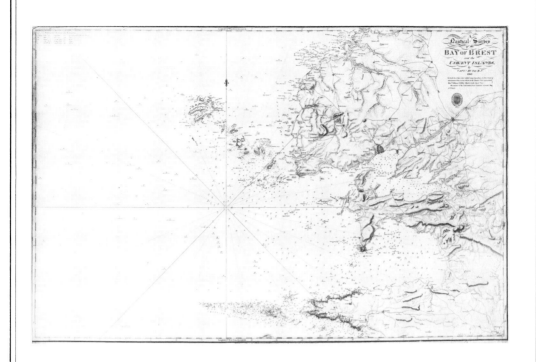

A Correct VIEW of the FRENCH FLAT-BOTTOM BOATS, intended to convey their TROOPS, for the INVASION of ENGLAND.

grateful adieu to the good sisters. They packed up a few trifles for my day's march and commended me to the commiseration of the guards. The French Midshipman shewed also towards me much kindness — indeed the attentions of all made me forget, while among them, that I was but a prisoner. The Hospitals in France may be considered as foremost in their Civil Institutions; nothing can surpass their cleanliness, good order, and tenderness to their sick. Under the superintendence of the sisters no kind of levity is admitted; and having the entire distribution of the provisions the diet of each is regulated to the case of the patient, and a degree of kindliness shewn him dictated by the tenderest benevolence. The Naval Hospital is a very large spacious building, but in a bad situation in the centre of the town. We were confined to what was termed 'the prison ward', and consequently restricted from going out — the only opportunity I had therefore of seeing the town of Brest was very limited — alone that of going to and from the Dock Yard. The streets through which I passed were very narrow, and the houses very high, built of a dark grey stone, which gave it a dark gloomy appearance — and the ramparts did not appear formidable, nor in the best state of repair, particularly on the side by which we were leaving the Town.

Before leaving Brest my small party of four men were joined by eleven poor culprits from the city prison. We were told by the *gens d'armes* that our two Deserters had entered into a Line-of-battle ship, and gave me to understand by a significant shrug that they were *mauvais sujets.*[9] The day's march though but eleven miles was to me uncommonly fatiguing, so little was I accustomed to marching. A little after noon we reached Landerneau a small but clean village and to my surprise were conducted with the poor people who accompanied us to the Bridewell[10], which was a small room up

Above: A view of Morlaix, where Hewson saw people busy making flat-bottomed boats for Napoleon's projected invasion of England. Hewson was confined for several days in the civil prison, formerly the Château du Taureau, built in 1542 at the harbour entrance to guard against any attack, such as the English fleet had made twenty years earlier.

Below: An artist's impression of the flat-bottomed boats in which Napoleon's army, assembled round Boulogne, was meant to invade England. Each boat, about 120 feet long and 40 broad, carried 500 men and was propelled by 18 sweeps on each side. The figure 1 marks the drawbridge in the bows for embarking and landing the troops.

a pair of stairs in a Miller's house, and so filthy as to be a receptacle for anything rather than man. When our fellow-travellers were unchained (a necessary precaution of the guards before taking them out in the morning, which we were not subject to) they greeted those whom they found in the prison as old friends. Soon after the Miller brought us up a loaf of bread which was our allowance for the day — in the evening some charity soup was brought to us: its mode of collection was that of placing a tub in the street every Sunday wherein each emptied their plates — but to such misery as now encircled me, it was great relief, and all ate with an appetite occasioned by want. Night closed this day's scene with a kind of nauseous feeling in my mind that conscious rectitude was unable to conquer. When rising from my straw in the morning, vermin were all over my clothes, which struck me with a pain not possible for Englishmen to conceive and too disgusting even at this length of time to describe.

We were now only to be marched on 'correspondence' days — a mode in France of transporting civil criminals through the Empire between the towns: at the distance of from twenty to thirty miles *gens d'armes* meet half-way at a certain hour and make an exchange of prisoners, and the number continually on the road truly surprises a stranger. The Brigadier or *Sergent* has a *file de route*, and all Police Correspondence, which they exchange, giving a regular receipt for prisoners, and all papers handed to each. Our stay at Landerneau was three days, and as before we were conducted to Landivisiau, and confined to a *Cachot* [prison cell] of the same filthy description as that of Landerneau. After two days' halt we again commenced our route for Morlaix, a longer march than either of the two former days, but we did not feel the fatigue so much. Our confinement was to the Civil Prison, where we had a yard to range in, one half of which was allotted to women. Hunger worked so powerfully on my men, that on the

A Broadside calling upon every Briton to resist the French invasion forces and the ambitions of Bonaparte, tyrant and assassin. The reference to Bonaparte poisoning thirty-three of his own soldiers and massacring four thousand Turks: after his army had stormed Jaffa in March 1799 he ordered the Turkish garrison plus another fourteen hundred prisoners to be put to death. When the French Army of the Orient reached Jaffa on its way to Acre, three hundred cases of bubonic plague were confined to hospital. On his return after being thwarted at Acre, Bonaparte gave orders that the remainder of the plague cases — perhaps sixty — be poisoned. His head doctor protested, and it is likely that the order was not carried out, because when the Turks arrived they found seven French soldiers alive.

Brave Soldiers,
Defenders of YOUR COUNTRY!

The road to glory is open before you—Pursue the great career of your Forefathers, and rival them in the field of honour. *A proud and usurping* TYRANT (a name ever execrated by Englishmen) dares to *threaten our shores with* INVASION, *and to reduce the free-born Sons of Britain to* SLAVERY *and* SERVITUDE! Forgetting what English Soldiers are capable of, and ranking them with the Hirelings of the Powers who have fallen his prey on the Continent, he supposes his threat easily executed. *Give him a lesson, my brave Countrymen, that he will not easily forget, and that France may have by heart for a Century to come!* Neither the vaunting Hero (who deserted his own Comrades and Soldiers in Egypt), nor the French Army, have ever been able to cope with British valour when fairly opposed to it. Our ancestors declared, that *ONE ENGLISHMAN was ever a match for* THREE FRENCHMEN—and that man to man was too great odds in our favour. We have but to feel their sentiments to confirm them;---you will find that their declaration was founded on experience; and that even in our day, within these three years, an army of your brave Comrades has convinced its admiring Country that the balance is still as great as ever against the enemy. *Our* EDWARD, *the illustrious Black Prince, laid waste the Country of France to the Gates of Paris, and on the Plains of Cressy left* 11 *Princes and* 30,000 *men dead upon the Field of Battle---a greater number than the whole English Army boasted at the beginning of the action.* The same heroic Prince, having annihilated the Fleet of France, *entirely routed her Army at Poictiers, took her King prisoner, and brought him Captive to London,* with thousands of his Nobles and People, and *all this against an Army* SIX TIMES AS NUMEROUS AS THAT OF THE ENGLISH! Did not our Harry the Fifth invade France, and at Agincourt *oppose an Army of* 9000 *men, sickly, fatigued, and half starved, to that of the French amounting to* 50,000: and did he not leave 10,000 of the enemy dead upon the field, and take 14,000 prisoners, with the loss of only 400 men?

Have we not, within this century, to boast a *MARLBOROUGH*, who (besides his other Victories) at Blenheim slew 12,000 of the French, and made 14,000 Prisoners, and *in less than a month conquered* 300 *miles of Territory from the Enemy?*

And are not the glories of our *ABERCROMBY and the gallant ARMY of EGYPT* fresh in your minds? *An Army of* 14,000 *Britons, who landed in the face of upwards of* 20,000 *troops of France, and drove from a country, with whose strong holds they were acquainted, and whose resources they knew how to apply, a host of Frenchmen enured to the climate, and veterans in arms? Did they not cut to pieces that vaunted Corps of Buonaparte's, whose successes against other Powers had obtained it the appellation of* INVINCIBLE—and is not their Standard (all that is left of it) a trophy at this moment in our Capital?

The Briton fights for his Liberty and Rights, the Frenchman fights for *Buonaparté,* who has robbed him of both! Which, then, in the nature of events, will be most zealous, most active, and most terrible in the Field of Battle?—the independent supporters of his country's cause, or the Slave who trembles lest the arms of his comrades should be turned against himself; who knows that his Leader, his General, his Tyrant, *did not hesitate, after having* MURDERED 4000 *disarmed Turks in cool blood, to* POISON 300 *of his own sick Soldiers, of men who had been fighting his battles of ambition, and been wounded in his defence.* English Soldiers will scarcely credit this, but it is on record not to be doubted, never to be expunged. But more; read and blush for the depravity even of an enemy. It is not that these bloody deeds were perpetrated from necessity, from circumstances however imperious at the moment; they were the acts of cool and deliberate determination, and his purpose, no less sanguinary, is again declared in the event of success in his enterprize against this Country. Feeling that even the slavish followers of his fortune were not to be forced to embark in this ruinous and destructive expedition, he declares to them in a public proclamation, or decoy, that *when they have landed in this Country, in order to make the booty the richer,* NO QUARTER *shall be given to the* BASE ENGLISH, *who fight for their perfidious Government---that they are to be* PUT TO THE SWORD, *and their Property distributed among the Soldiers of the Victorious Army!!!* Say is this the conduct of a Hero? is this the man who is destined to break the spirit of Englishmen? *shall we suffer an* ASSASSIN *to enter our blessed Country, and despoil our fields of their produce---to massacre our brave Soldiers in cool blood, and hang up every man who has carried arms?* Your cry is Vengeance for the insult—and vengeance is in your own hands. It must be signal and terrible! Like the bolt from Heaven let it strike the devoted Army of Invaders! *Every Frenchman will find his Grave where he first steps on British ground, and not a Soldier of Buonaparte's boasted Legions shall escape the fate his ambitious Tyrant has prepared for him!*

Britons Strike Home!
Or your Fame is for ever blasted,—your Liberties for ever lost!!!

Printed for J. GINGER, 169, Piccadilly; Price 6d. a Dozen for distribution; by D. N. SHURY, Berwick Street, Soho,

PUBLICOLA.

road they bartered by turns the few clothes I got them at Brest for meat and wine — as for myself the change of diet to only brown bread caused a total want of appetite. Sickness ensued, which weakened me very much. We took advantage of a long halt at Morlaix to wash our shirts, and be again prepared for marching. The country through which we passed between Morlaix and Brest was no further interesting than such scenes generally are to sailors that have been any time afloat, who when chance brings them on shore look on barren rocks with delight. I had been in constant active service from the moment of my entering into the Navy, and had not been on shore even through the short interval of peace, & of course all bore to me a smiling aspect, though the country was very barren, and not having one appearance of comfort. On entering Landerneau all was a scene of gaudy gaiety, being Sunday. The women were in their fineries, and there were one or two dancing parties in the street. Landivisiau was a very miserable village — but Morlaix was a very nice town — and all the people were alive building *Bâteaux plats* for the invasion of England[11]: 'twas a place which formerly had a great deal of communication with England in the exchange of 'cartels'[12], but its harbour would only admit vessels of small draught of water.

On Monday Octr. 9th we again commenced our march, accompanied by a large party of culprits, among whom were two or three women, under an escort of *gens d'armes*: our road led at times by the sea-shore, which indeed occasioned an anxious desire to escape from our conductors, and when at length finally leaving the sea-shore, I felt a depression of spirits as if doomed for some time to a forced absence from a profession to which I was ardently attached: though I then little expected the very long imprisonment awaiting me. At about seven o'clock we reached Lannion, a small but neat town, and the country somewhat more improved. The guards had been more diligent this day than ordinary: we were very tired and weary from the heat of the day, and instantly threw ourselves on our straw, on being locked in our cell. I soon became acquainted with the gaoler's daughters, who for the pride of showing that they spoke a little English were not distant. Three hundred English prisoners had for some time been in depôt[13] at this place, & seemed to have left a favourable impression at least on the feelings of the fair daughters of the gaoler, who amused me much with many anecdotes of them. A bundle of straw with our bread as usual was served to us.

At daylight the following morning we again marched out having an addition of seven or eight women to our party: and in the evening came to a very poor village where men and women were all confined to the same

Cachot, and among such unhappy people the scene of the night may be conceived well. Two or three of the *gens d'armes* under no control of gaolkeeper, or rather excited by him to encourage a free libation of his spirits, came to the room to partake of the revelry. When the morning came, to my relief, the same parties again marched. This day it rained incessantly, and the guards behaved towards us very unfeelingly. When we halted to change correspondence, as we could not afford to pay for a little wine, we were one and all turned into a yard at the public-house.

At night we reached Guingamp very much fatigued. On entering the prison-yard the savoury fumes of some Bullock's liver, which one of the prisoners was stewing, most powerfully attracted our notice, and our first act was to barter one of our loaves of bread for some of it, and I don't know when I was more regaled, which none but those who have endured a long abstinence from meat could suppose. Our present abode had formerly been a monastery, and was yet in its highest state of preservation — its piazzas turned into booths or small workshops by the prisoners where many worked at their various trades, and some were selling goods in their shops and seemed as if regularly to have taken up their abode there — indeed it was pleasing to see in such a seeming scene of misery and distress that Industry, and its natural attendant, moral conduct, existed. The French have the happiest possible mode of reconciling to themselves every attribute of crime, and under every circumstance being cheerful and merry. I seldom saw anything of depraved conduct in the large prisons — on the contrary a great degree of deference of manner, as among a well regulated society: but the abominable *Cachots* in the small villages were the extreme of all that was filth.

After leaving Guingamp, a room in the yard of a shoemaker's shop became our next abode, where a large Dog at our door served for Keeper during the night. Our halt was five days in this wretched place. About thirty of us were locked up in this small room — at night lying heads and tails, and not having room even to turn on our straw, with no air but what the crevices admitted. Our leaving this hole was truly a relief, and it must be equally so to my readers — my only saying that our various sufferings during the remainder of our route through Brittany would be but a monotonous repetition of the past.

When we changed correspondence one day, the Brigadier of the relieving guard asked me if I spoke French, and being answered in jest by those who accompanied me that I could sometimes make myself understood, he immediately took out his chain (a *garment* they always kept in their

43

Guingamp, from a drawing by Benoit. It shows the Basilica of Notre-Dame-de-Bon-Secours and the River Trieux. Hewson arrived here under escort on 11 October 1803, and was held in a former monastery.

pockets) and linked me to those of their train — some of whom perhaps were going for trial for murder, and others to slavery. My mind was overpowered by such an act of humiliation towards a British prisoner of war, and in sullen silence I suffered myself to be dragged along. The same cruel treatment was persevered in from that moment, though I was so enfeebled from fatigue and bad food that I scarcely had strength to perform the day's marches, and would never have succeeded but that the poor people as we passed through the villages would give us a little cider or milk on their hearing that we were English. At last we reached Rennes and were conducted to the well-known Tour de Balle, which was conspicuous in the centre of the town, far above the houses at some distance from it. Here we were led to believe would cease a deal of the strict guard of the *gens d'armes* in consequence of the good feelings of the Bretagnes [Bretons] for the English — indeed the *gens d'armes* spoke of the people through Brittany, as being *demi-barbares*, and always looked on them with contempt, as if not at all connected by any tie of country.

The morning after our reaching Rennes I was taken very ill and a fever ensued occasioned by want of food and the severe marching. I was obliged to apply through the gaolkeeper to the Commissary of War to be removed to the Hospital as being no longer able to march, which he most inhumanly refused, but directed that a cart should be provided for those that were unable to march, on which among some other sick people going the same correspondence, I was ordered a place. Through Brittany we were allowed 3 lbs. of bread: it was now reduced to 1½ lbs., in lieu of which we were given three sous on the days alone that we marched. My little party was joined here by a Guernsey man calling himself Captain of a vessel taken at St. Malo. As he spoke French I hoped to find him of great assistance to us, and meeting any one being a subject of England our feelings warmed towards him.

Now entering France, which the *gens d'armes* were telling us was the land of liberty, we were relieved from the torture of the chains and handcuffs, and the *gens d'armes* at once seemed to throw off their suspicious watch of us, but we did not meet with the same kindliness from

Foot *gendarmes* of the period 1800–10. The men wore a deep blue long-tailed coat with red facings. A red plume adorned the felt cocked hat. This picture shows one *gendarme* in trousers, the other in fawn breeches with knee-length gaiters. Each is armed with a flintlock musket, bayonet and side arm.

GENDARME À CHEVAL.

the people in passing through the villages — however being relieved from the degradation of the chains which seemed to proceed from distrust, my spirits were again animated. The appearance of the villages began to resemble those of England in cleanliness, and the prisons, or rather *cachots*, bore a striking contrast to those we passed — they were comfortable in comparison — for the thought of such receptacles for our fellow-creatures is painful in the extreme to the mind.

To give a particular narrative of each halt would be tiresome — in some prisons we met with gentle treatment — at others a wanton severity — but as we had but our three halfpence to spend, we could not extort that smile, which more than half feeds the hungry.

I shall not pass over Laval; the morning of our leaving which place we were told that our allowance of bread would be given to us on reaching our night's halt — but here we were told that they never keep bread for prisoners, nor did we get any till getting to our following night's halt: thus travelling a distance of sixty miles without sustenance was a severity unheard of towards my poor men.

The want of food and being continually kept in motion, as the correspondence was more regular than in Brittany, soon ridded me of my fever — a good constitution prevailed over every privation, but I was very weak, and but for the assistance of the cart would not have been enabled to march.

On our road to Chartres the *gens d'armes* took us through the village of Rockford where a Mr. Johnstone an Irish gentleman who was joined in a cotton factory received us most humanely, giving us our breakfast, and seeing the bare state of my poor men ordered his old clothes to be divided amongst them — nor can I in gratitude pass over a generous son of the same nation, a workman of the manufactory whose small means not answering to the largeness of his heart, ran out to the villagers, and by begging and borrowing among them caused so much sympathy, that when we returned to our cart from Mr. Johnstone's we found it stuffed with old clothes, shoes, old hats, &c. and he himself went tick with the baker for a sufficiency of bread to serve us for four or five days. When the mind is depressed by a long series of suffering every sensitive organ is susceptible to the slightest touch of commiseration, so this poor man's method of

A mounted *gendarme*. They also wore a deep blue uniform, fawn breeches, and cocked hat. Their weapons comprised a carbine and a heavy cavalry sword.

relieving us awakened every power in my soul to express — I was ambitious of being a Prince that I might reward his generous heart.

From Chartres I wrote my brother George and Mr. Lapenotiere, the Commander of the *Pickle* Schooner, and enclosed my letters to Mr. Johnstone, who was kind enough to say that he would forward them for me. As we advanced towards Paris I was getting quite strong and in as good health as I had enjoyed for some time. The Guernsey Captain was made caterer of our small subsistence money which was generally expended at the first *auberge* for wine. The idea of having a person with us who could speak French made me meditate on effecting my escape with some of my men: and as I began to recover in my health I was daily communicating my plans to the Guernsey man, who gave me reason to believe that he was equally anxious to undertake it. The day after leaving Chartres, but one *gen d'armes* accompanied us, whom the good wine at our halt induced to take more freely of than exactly tempered with his duty, which offered us the fairest opportunity of putting it into execution, and which the generous conduct of Mr. Johnstone in changing an English five-pound note for one of my men, more particularly put in our power to effect — but to my surprise this *ci-devant* Captain had the baseness not only to refuse joining us, but threatened if we made any movement that he would have us stopped, saying, 'that he had high destinies assigned him, & was employed on secret service'. I afterwards met this poor man confined to one of the *souterrains* in Bitche employed as a spy on his fellow-prisoners.

Each day's march offered us something new, but not of sufficient interest to relate. Approaching towards Paris the winter was setting in — the harvest was all housed — the leaves falling from the trees, and cold northern blasts, with rains setting in. It was always night before our marches terminated — very frequently dripping wet, and turned to a cold cell or *cachot* without clothes with which to shift and only a pound and half of straw each to rest our wearied limbs on during the night. Though no difference of treatment was shewn towards me by the French Authorities, yet I was doubly compensated by the uncommon respect paid me by my poor men who on all occasions referred to me their various causes of complaint and grievances. As a necessary preservative to health, whenever water could be procured in the prisons, I obliged them to wash their things, and as an example always took off my own shirt first — my whole stock consisting but of what I stood in, for I had the misfortune to lose my small package containing the shirt and stockings which I got at Brest out of the cart. Notwithstanding every means within our reach to preserve our strength Ino. Humphries got sick from the damps of the prisons, and when we reached Melun had the gaol distemper so bad that I was obliged to apply to the Commissary of War to have him removed to the Hospital and was myself allowed to be one of his conductors, and parted with him with some pain commending him to the care of the sisters.

At a small village at which we halted after leaving Melun, we were again agreeably visited by a countryman, who disengaged himself from a party in the woods (being Sunday) to spend the afternoon with us: he brought with him his wife, his leg of mutton, and a few bottles of wine, the cheering influence of which made us forget the iron bars which enclosed us.

On leaving Brest we were told that we should be conducted to Fontaine-bleau, but at Melun, only one day's march from our depôt, our destination was changed for Verdun, in the department of the Meuse, which was yet sixty leagues [about 180 miles] from us. This was a great disappointment to us as we had been looking forward to a speedy termination to our fatigues.

We had not left Melun more than three or four days, when I had a return of the Fever, or gaol distemper, accompanied by very severe rheumatic pains, occasioned by continually being in wet clothes, and damp cells, which in a short time so weakened me that I was forced to allow myself to be carried from the straw in the cell to the cart when marching and actually became so helpless that I could in no way assist myself. Often have I known us marching from dawn of day till two hours after dark, under continued rains, & when we were halted at the village for the purpose of exchanging correspondence, or feeding their horses, unless we might have a few sous from our allowance to spend, the *gens d'armes* would turn us into an open yard very frequently for two or three hours, until they had paid their respective visits to the *bonnes amies*: when the well-known sound of 'Allons, bougres Anglais! Marchons!' would rouse us from the shelter of the wall. Then at night entering a cold damp cell frequently streaming with drains of saltpetre water — but forced to lie down to rest our spent limbs would as soon be covered with vermin — the moment of dawn of day again to rise and disburthen our clothes of their unwelcome inmates and be prepared for the *gens d'armes*.

In some prisons where we would be halted for the day they would turn us into the yard until evening — then serve us our two pounds and half of straw each, and lock us up — at some places this pittance of straw was refused to prisoners of war. When we reached Chaumont en Bassigny the *gens d'armes* procured an order for me to be admitted into the Hospital, being so helpless from my pains they would no longer be delayed on their

A view of Melun, which is built on the banks of the Seine and on an island in the river. It was here that Hewson learnt that his destination was to be Verdun instead of Fontainebleau.

marches by me. I parted from my crew with very great pain. They maintained to the last their attention to me, and I felt assured that they were sincere in their sorrow at my leaving them — for I did all in my power to protect them from imposition at the *haut ton* of the *gens d'armes*.

Behold me once more at the Military Hospital supplied with clean things, wholesome food, and everything I could desire, and which ought to have at once contributed to have restored me to health — but during the first week the fever much increased and at times I was delirious — but it pleased the Lord again to spare me.

The Doctor kept me to my bed more than a month, but when I was at length allowed to walk about, I took as much exercise as confinement to the Hospital would admit. I did not long enjoy the hope of recovering health. The rheumatic pains returned, and increased so much I was obliged to keep my bed. Again my limbs enflamed, and I could not move but in the most excruciating pain, and became so helpless that I could not feed myself. In this melancholy state I continued for some weeks. I lost all appetite, and now indeed felt great depression of spirit — not from the thought of an approaching end, but at departing this life without the comfort of a burial in the Protestant faith. Oh! had I known then the true merits of a Redeemer, such thoughts would not have disturbed my peace.

To my great surprise and no less joy, Ino. Humphries, the seaman whom I left in Melun Hospital, was brought to this Hospital. He recovered from the Fever in which I left him, and was again sent forward on his march, but they detained him so long in the prison of Chaumont (that in the idea of my recovery to accompany him we should be marched together to Verdun) that he got the gaol distemper a second time, and which occasioned him to be sent to the Hospital.

The Commissary of War came to inspect our wards and was much surprised that no money had been given me for subsistence on the road more than what had been granted to the men, and promised when I was sufficiently recovered to proceed on my march that he would give me three

In this letter dated 30 January 1804 and addressed to Sir Evan Nepean, Secretary of the Admiralty, Captain Thomas Elphinstone, commanding HMS *Diamond*, describes how Maurice Hewson was taken prisoner by the French at Brest. 'I have therefore to request you will be pleased to signify the same to their Lordships that I may know their pleasure whether I am to discharge Mr Hewson from the Books of this Ship or continue him Borne for Wages.'

His Majesty's Ship Diamond
at Spithead 3rd January 1804

Copy E 116

Sir

Mr. Marn. Hewson a Midn.
belonging to His Majesty's Ship under
my Command, having been sent into Port
as Prize Master was afterwards sent on
board His Majesty's Schooner Pickle for a
passage in order to join this Ship at Sea
but while the Pickle was reconnoitring in shore
near Brest he was despatched in one of her
Boats in pursuit of a French Fishing Boat
and was taken a Prisoner

I have therefore to request you
will be pleased to signify the same to their
Lordships that I may know their pleasure
whether I am to discharge Mr. Hewson
from the Books of this Ship or continue him
Borne for Wages.

I have the Honor to be
Sir
Your Most Obedient
Humble Servant

Thos. Elphinstone

To Sir Evan Nepean Bart.
Admiralty Office London

livres a day, and that he would direct that I should no longer be confined to the Prisons, but sent to the Inns — and though indeed in a very weak state under this promise I begged him to order my march as soon as possible. Not feeling at all any hope of recovery I determined to make a struggle to get to Verdun and on the sixth of January [1804] the *gens d'armes* came for me and I was carried to a cart by some of the men who scarcely believed they bore a living creature. The good sister of the hospital had previously furnished me with a pair of warm worsted stockings and shoes, my own being worn out, and also gave me a little sweet wine and some white bread. I gave her all I had in return, my blessing, which I trust may have gone up on high, and, with a heart overflowing with remembrance of her many kind attentions to me, set off with Humphries, & several poor conscripts. It was a cold and frosty morning and the cart over a rough road shook me very much, but the fresh air revived me and when we came to a halt I got a little Pork Soup, and something for Humphries, which added to the hope of a clean bed at night at an Inn — but in this I was disappointed and *malgré moi* once more forced to pay my humble respects to the honorable Governor of a Prison, where, from a few compliments to his fireside, cleanliness of his room, &c. and what acted still more instinctively, a hint from the *gens d'armes* that I had subsistence money allowed me for the road, I was shewn to a bed, most miserable indeed, for 24 sous, though at an *auberge* it would not exceed six.

When the Commissary in his generous feeling directed three *livres* to be given me for the marching day's expense, he did not calculate on the days of halt for correspondence which was frequently a week, and for which time I had nothing on which to subsist, and having spent some cash in a little soup, and something for Humphries, the previous day, my little money was near its last farthing. In the fore part of the day, the gaoler's wife came to me with a smiling countenance, and full of the morning compliments, and I equally put on my best looks to meet her civilities, and told her that the bed caused me much ease from my pains, though during the night I had been feverish from the fatigue of the previous day, and drank a great quantity of water. She apologised to me for not leaving me better than water to drink, saying I should have spoken before going to bed. From her commiseration I thought that I had been severe in my opinion of her. After some little time she said she was in a hurry, and 'as you are not going to get up, I want you to pay for the bed'. I told her that I had settled it with her husband the night before — she said that was but for the night, and I would equally use the bed by laying on it during the day. I assured her of my inability to discharge her second price, but her inhuman heart was not to be moved. I was lifted from the bed by her and her husband who came to her assistance, not having strength of myself to move, and was laid on the floor till night.

Our next march was to Joinville where I was no sooner shewn to my cell than some of the many inmates of the prison came to make me pay my entrance money, & actually threatened to beat me with the soles of their shoes, for non-compliance: in fact, though but through three more prisons before reaching Verdun, I met in each most inhuman & unmanly treatment, which now only excites pity. Suffice it to say that on the fourteenth day I reached Verdun very ill, and therefore chose going to the Hospital, where in my destitute state I might hope for more suitable means for my recovery than I could look for in lodgings by myself.

PRISONNIERS DE GUERRE ANGLAIS.

Dépôt de Verdun.

ORDRE DE POLICE

Du Général Commandant Supérieur en cette Place, donné en exécution des ordres de S. E. le Ministre de la Guerre, des 1.er Germinal an 12 et 30 Mars 1809.

Verdun, 1.er Avril 1809.

L'INSPECTEUR-GÉNÉRAL au Corps Impérial de la Gendarmerie, l'un des Commandans de la Légion d'Honneur, Commandant Supérieur à Verdun, ayant la grande Police sur les Prisonniers de Guerre *Anglais* du Dépôt établi en cette Place,

Ordonne l'envoi, à toutes les Brigades de Gendarmerie stationnées dans le Département de la Meuse, du Réglement de Police ci-après, dont lesdites Brigades assureront, en ce qui les concerne, l'exécution.

ARTICLE 1.er

CONFORMÉMENT à l'article 10 du Réglement approuvé par S. E. le Ministre de la Guerre, le 17 Nivose an 12,

Nul Prisonnier de Guerre, admis au régime de la parole d'honneur, ne peut être dispensé de se trouver aux jours et heures fixés pour les appels de sa classe.

ART. 2.

Il ne peut être accordé d'exemptions d'appels que dans un seul cas, celui de maladie qui oblige le Prisonnier de garder le lit ou la chambre; et, dans ce cas, l'état du malade doit être certifié par une déclaration écrite de l'Officier de Santé Français en exercice près le Dépôt, et représentée à l'Officier Commandant le Détachement de Gendarmerie Impériale, toujours avant la clôture des appels.

Cet Officier de Santé est M.r Juzay, Médecin de l'Hôpital Militaire de Verdun.

ART. 3.

Indépendamment de la représentation de ces certificats, l'Officier de Gendarmerie ordonnera à un Sous-Officier de s'assurer, tous les jours, de la situation du Prisonnier malade et de sa présence à son logement.

ART. 4.

S'il est reconnu que le Prisonnier, auquel il a été délivré un certificat de maladie, n'était pas dans l'impossibilité de paraître aux appels, l'Officier de Santé qui en aura signé le certificat ne pourra plus être cru dans aucun cas, et il sera rendu compte de cet abus au Général Commandant Supérieur.

ART. 5.

Tout Prisonnier de Guerre qui, hors le cas de légitime dispense prévu ci-dessus, ne se sera pas trouvé aux appels de sa classe, sera considéré comme ayant manqué à sa parole d'honneur, et mis à la Citadelle jusqu'à nouvel ordre.

ART. 6.

Tout Sous-Officier ou Gendarme du Détachement qui sera convaincu d'avoir faussement attesté qu'un Prisonnier s'est trouvé aux appels, sa maladie, ou la présence du Prisonnier à son logement, sera mis sur-le-champ en prison. Sa destitution sera provoquée par un rapport à S. E. le Maréchal d'Empire, premier Inspecteur-Général de l'arme.

L'Officier Commandant le Détachement qui, après le recensement général des appels, en aura certifié l'exactitude sur les états qui seront remis au Commandant Supérieur, en sera, dès ce moment, responsable. Il est enjoint à cet Officier de porter sur-le-champ, à la connaissance de l'autorité supérieure, les abus, malversations, négligences et inexactitudes qu'il y aura reconnus dans toutes les parties du service dont il est chargé.

ART. 7.

Tout Prisonnier de Guerre sur parole, ayant permission de sortir des portes, qui franchira la distance d'un rayon de deux lieues en dehors de la Place de Verdun,

sans l'autorisation par écrit du Commandant Supérieur, manque à son engagement d'honneur. Dans ce cas, non seulement la Gendarmerie, les Maires des Communes et leurs Adjoints, la Garde Nationale, les Gardes Forestiers et les Gardes Ruraux, mais encore, tout Citoyen a le droit d'arrêter ledit Prisonnier, sauf à le remettre aussi-tôt à la disposition de la Brigade de Gendarmerie la plus rapprochée, ou du Maire de la Commune, pour que son transferement, sous sûre escorte, ait lieu, sans retard, dans la Place de Verdun. Le Prisonnier de Guerre sera d'abord mis à la Citadelle, et sa permission lui sera retirée.

ART. 8.

Il est expressément défendu d'exercer aucun mauvais traitement envers les Prisonniers de Guerre arrêtés dans le cas prévu par l'article 7, qui ne feront aucune difficulté de suivre l'escorte qui les ramènera dans la Place. Ceux desdits Prisonniers qui refuseront de marcher devront y être contraints. En cas de mutinerie, rébellion ou résistance à la Garde Nationale ou à la Gendarmerie, il en sera dressé procès-verbal, d'après lequel les Prévenus seront traduits, s'il y a lieu, devant une Commission Militaire, conformément au Decret Impérial du 17 Frimaire an 14, promulgué au Dépôt de Verdun le 15 Avril 1806.

Tout Gendarme qui se portera à des excès envers un Prisonnier de Guerre, qui le maltraitera, exigera de lui la plus légère rétribution, qui, hors le cas de mutinerie, de résistance à l'exécution d'un ordre légal, ou de légitime défense, emploiera des moyens de rigueur et de force, sera sévèrement puni.

ART. 9.

Le présent Ordre sera envoyé au Capitaine Commandant la Gendarmerie du Département de la Meuse, qui demeure chargé de le transmettre à toutes les Brigades de cette Compagnie. Les Sous-Officiers Commandant ces Brigades s'entendront avec les Maires des Communes, les Commandans de la Garde Nationale, les Gardes Forestiers et Ruraux de leurs arrondissemens respectifs, lesquels seront invités et pourront, en besoin, être requis, dans les termes de la Loi du 28 Germinal an 6, article 157 et suivans, de concourir avec la Gendarmerie à l'exécution de ces dispositions, qui auront lieu à l'égard des Prisonniers de Guerre arrêtés au-delà du rayon de deux lieues sans permission pour franchir cette distance.

ART. 10.

Une gratification de cinquante francs est accordée par le Gouvernement pour la capture de chaque Prisonnier de Guerre sur parole qui, étant arrêté en dehors du rayon de deux lieues de la place de Verdun, y sera ramené et remis à la disposition de l'autorité militaire.

ART. 11.

Afin que le présent Ordre de Police soit connu de tous ceux qui doivent concourir à son exécution, il sera imprimé à un nombre suffisant d'exemplaires, pour, à la diligence de chaque Commandant de Brigade, être affiché aux portes principales de l'Église paroissiale et de la Mairie de chaque Commune dans le Département de la Meuse.

Signé, G.al WIRION.

II

Life as a Prisoner in Verdun

THE scene was indeed changed, having now my fellow-countrymen and brother-officers continually coming in and out, and their cheerful conversation was a restoring balm to my worn-out spirits. There were two young gentlemen of the *Shannon* Frigate confined to their beds near me, which Frigate had been wrecked on the Saints' Rocks off Brest[14] some time after my departure from that place, but being marched direct for Verdun under merely an escort and not confined for a day, and allowed on their march to occupy the Inns, had arrived some time before me at Verdun. Captain Gore[15] who commanded her and all his officers who were on parole occasionally came in to see the young gentlemen who were in the ward, but my shattered appearance did not create much sympathy in them, indeed one of my fellow-inmates would scarcely acknowledge me.

I now had truly reason to fall down prostrate before the God of Mercies for his preservation through such a march and bringing me to a place where I might say I had kindred friends, and every hope of alleviation. In the evening I was visited by Mr. Fennell, first Lieutenant of the *Minerve* commanded by Captain Brenton[16], also wrecked off Cherbourg since my captivity. He told me that Captain Brenton had gone to Givet, and left him to superintend the depôt — that he was authorised to furnish all gentlemen coming to the depôt in distress till they were enabled to provide for themselves, and would feel a pleasure in being of service to me. I told him the particulars of my capture — the imprisonment I underwent at Brest — my near escape of being tried by a Court Martial for my life in consequence of the testimony of the two deserters — my having been more than five

Orders to the *gendarmerie* from the Commandant of the Verdun depot dated 1 April 1809. They concern roll call, the supervision of sick prisoners of war, the penalties for any police who abuse their powers, and the Government reward of 50 francs payable to anyone who recaptures and hands over to the police any prisoner of war who has broken his parole.

months on the road, with only the subsistence of a pound and half of bread, and three sous, the days I marched, till the last twenty-five leagues — that from the cold damps of the prisons, and from having been marched in such severe weather without sufficient sustenance, my constitution was much worn, and such were my necessities that I was indebted to the Hospital for the shirt I wore. I told him also of my ability to draw on my friends, and that I should feel the obligation most warmly, could he get me a bill cashed for Ten Pounds, or let me have half that sum till I might be enabled to get out of the Hospital when my first object would be to repay him. He regretted not having then so much about him, but would bring it me in the morning. He kindly stopped with me half an hour commiserating my sufferings, and on leaving me again repeated his promise. The following evening Mr. Fennell called but only with an apology for forgetting me — the moment he went home, he said, he would put the money in his pocket for me. A few days passed, and some seamen came to the Hospital whom he came to see: and as he was passing the foot of my bed I spoke to him telling him that the surgeon ordered me medicines that the Hospital did not allow, which I must provide for myself. His excuses were too numerous to be repeated — they were as empty as his heart was pitiless, nor did I again see him for a fortnight when he came with his accustomed condolences, and to ask me if Captain Brenton had been to see me for he had returned from Givet more than a week. I was so very much hurt at his neglect towards me that with pain I could make him a civil answer. I could not account for such conduct in making proffers of relief without any intention to fulfil them.

Nothing could be more attentive to me than the surgeon of the Hospital — he so well understood my case that I soon began to feel the good effects of his treatment. In about a month the fever quite left me, and I was allowed to sit up in my bed a few hours in each day. One afternoon Dr. Allen of the *Minerve* passing my bed to visit some seamen in the ward on seeing me asked was I an Englishman, — and was surprised that he did not before hear of my being in Town — he was certain that Mr. Fennell could not have mentioned me to Captain Brenton, and had the goodness to go at the moment to him, with whom he shortly returned. I repeated to Captain Brenton what I had related to Mr. Fennell of my captivity and sufferings, begging to be excused for not sooner reporting myself to him — but that I believed Mr. Fennell had already done so. He felt all that a good heart could express, and assured me of his protection and assistance and that evening sent me five Pounds — and his uniform kindness to me during his stay in the depôt will ever be gratefully remembered by me. Dr. Allen recommended to me warm baths, the good effects of which I soon began to feel by recovering once more the use of my limbs. To be enabled to stand after so long a confinement to my bed was cause of Thanksgiving to the Almighty — the more so when looking back to the day of my removal from Chaumont one of the *sergents* hearing me moaning under very great pain said 'I would never again dare visit their shores'. When I was able to walk it was a great delight to me going to the garden and amusing myself with its varieties — my brother officers came in often to see me and much amused me by the strange Jokes of John Bull.

Towards the latter end of March I found myself sufficiently recovered to leave the Hospital with a Master of a Merchant Vessel who joined me in taking two small rooms. Being both invalids, we mutually assisted each other, and formed a mess. The maidservant purchased for us the little we wanted from market and during my *séjour* at Verdun, I certainly never was happier, and never passed a more peaceable time, than with this honest and worthy man. Before my leaving the Hospital Michael Connors who was one of the deserters with the Boat at Brest, and had caused all my sufferings, made his *entrée* among us. I learned that he had been in a Line-of-Battle Ship at Brest, but in consequence of his ill-conduct was turned on shore, and sent after his ship-mates to a depôt. I begged Dr. Allen to report him to Captain Brenton who hesitated not in going to Genl. Wirion[17] in order to have him removed to Bitche as not deserving liberty. When the *gens d'armes* went for him, he volunteered for the Irish Brigade[18]. Some time after his fellow-mate was sent the same route, and on hearing the just detestation in which Connors was held entered also in the same Brigade.

The liberty of going about the Town and walking in the country at certain hours by a permit which Captain Brenton obtained made Verdun a paradise to me — it was such a contrast to what I had been lately enduring. The daily arrivals of English gentlemen from all parts of France where they had been detained previous to the commencement of the War gave an air of importance to the depôt, and caused a circulation of fashion & splendor rarely to be met with even at watering-places in England: but I purposely avoided forming any acquaintance but those whom my honest Captain might introduce, whom he now and then bid to join in our evening's chat. As soon as I could walk without assistance, the variety of the country, and fishing, afforded me great amusement — and when at home my hours were occupied in the study of French.

I passed two months in this quiet retired way, hardly knowing the time passing, when the surgeon's Assistant of the *Hussar* Frigate[19] (which was

also just wrecked on the coast, and whose officers were marched to Verdun) came to entreat to be admitted a member of our mess. In order to accommodate him it was necessary for us to remove to larger rooms. The son of a Dartmouth Merchant who was known to my club likewise joined us.

By mere accident I learned one day that my cousin Lieutenant Thos. Croasdaile [Crosdale] of the Navy was among the detained prisoners. On my going to see him I found him very ill of a brain fever: however he immediately knew me, and I don't think any two liberated from the Fleet Prison[20] returning to their wives and children could have felt more joy at meeting, though under such painful auspices. Dr. Jackson who attended him had a consultation the day before on his state, and such was the state of his pulse that they had but small hopes of his recovery; however in about a week it pleased the Lord to cause a favourable turn, and spare him to his family. I was constantly by his bed scarcely leaving him till he got considerably better. In my care of him, I was assisted by his good landlady, who watched with affection his most trifling call: frequently he was delirious, and would call for his dear mother — 'Alors, Monsr., je pleurs comme un enfant. Je ne puis me tenir, et je l'embrasse comme s'il était mon

Above: An interior view of Verdun from the ramparts. It shows the River Meuse and the Cathedral, which was consecrated in 1147 and damaged by fire in 1755. Opposite the west end stands the Bishop's Palace.

The drawing was made by James Forbes (1749–1819), who spent twenty years in the service of the East India Company. In 1803, when the Peace of Amiens was broken, he was detained at Verdun, but was released in the following year. His *Letters from France*, published in 1806, gave a misleading and unduly favourable picture of life and conditions for the *détenus* and the prisoners of war. Forbes later wrote *Oriental Memoirs*.

Below: The wreck of HMS *Magnificent* (74 guns) on 25 March 1804 on the Black Rocks off the Ile de Béniquet west of Brest. It was while helping to save the crew that Hewson's schoolfellow Christopher Tuthill from HMS *Impétueux* was captured. A new ship *Magnificent* was launched in the Thames in 1806. Hewson served in her as Lieutenant from 1809 to 1812.

The painting is by John Christian Schetky (1778–1874), who was marine painter in ordinary to George IV, William IV and Queen Victoria.

A lithograph by Hostein of Verdun and the Meuse. On the left is the Cathedral, on the right the Church of St Pierre and the fourteenth-century Porte Chaussée. The Citadel, where prisoners of war were confined, lies away to the left.

fils' — such was the tenderness of her feeling when thinking of his distance from his friends.

About the month of July my old schoolfellow Mr. Christopher Tuthill had the misfortune to be made prisoner in assisting to save the crew from the wreck of H. M. Ship *Magnificent*. With him and Mr. Thorley[21] his shipmate I now joined in a mess, substituting one of my honest Captain's Dartmouth friends in my place who had just arrived. This was an arrangement more congenial to my feelings.

We had our dinners sent to us from a *Traiteur*[22], under covers, for the small sum of fifteen sous each, and lived really very comfortably. We had a French master to attend us, and learning French was the order of the day. In these economical habits of life I found I could support myself with respect for Thirty Pounds a-year with the addition of Twenty Eight *Livres* allowed us by the French Government. Through the kindness of the Revd. Mr. L. Lee I was enabled to procure money at no great trouble for my Bills. The Revd. Launcelot Chas. Lee was an English Clergyman who, having been travelling in France at the period of the war breaking out, was included in the general arrest. To this gentleman I was greatly indebted for his uniform kindness in always endorsing my Bills. He was much esteemed & respected at Verdun. My friend Barklimore informed me that he died at his living in Oxfordshire in 1842. Those who had but their subsistence for their support, suffered the greatest privations and difficulties: 'twas only by living four in a double-bedded room which served at same time as kitchen, going to market each in his turn, that they were enabled to exist, and even with all this management, it did not suffice to clothe them. These pecuniary embarrassments led many deserving young men to associate with low company, and contract habits of drinking and gambling — the consequences of which were arrears of rent and occasional visits to the Town Gaol: but the class most to be commiserated were the Masters of Merchantmen who having but the same subsistence were obliged to have recourse to their

Above: The frigate *Hussar*, in which Hewson's friend O'Brien served as Master's Mate, was wrecked near Ushant (now the Ile d'Ouessant) on 8 February 1804. The ship's company, less her Captain, made Brest harbour by superb seamanship and surrendered to French warships there.

Below: Another drawing of Verdun by James Forbes, made from Telegraph Hill just outside the town.

small savings in England — when that was exhausted they were necessitated to go to service, and their families in England who from being accustomed to live in the ease and comfort of an honest industry, now from the long and severe imprisonment of the husband and father driven to the heartrending necessity of claiming relief from their parishes — some there were from a compassionate feeling towards them would suffer under every pang of want rather than take from their babes and wife. Such was my honest Dartmouth Captain — nor was there a hope when such surrounding complaints might be relieved by an exchange.

At Verdun there was I suppose the greatest jumble and admixture of character among the *détenus*, ever collected in so small a space. It consisted of about Eight Hundred, including all ranks, in the depôt, unknown to each other, but by the general misfortune — so that whatever might have been their former standing in society, or whatever the cause of absenting themselves from their country, 'twas unknown to their fellow-lodgers, and an opportunity given of wearing the garb of integrity — some among them, those who were in necessity, were most liberally provided for by a patriotic fund at Lloyd's[23], but the major part were men of property, and some with

An engraving of the Seal for Lloyd's Patriotic Fund, founded in July 1803.

Committee Room,
Lloyd's Coffee House,

I am directed by the Committee respectfully to recommend to your attention the annexed, which announces the necessity of a New Subscription for the Relief of the British Prisoners in France.

The Committee beg leave to state that the last Subscription, amounting to £30,000, has been applied during three years in administering Relief to upwards of 6000 of the Prisoners, and has, according to advices from the very respectable Gentlemen who were employed in France to select the proper objects at the different Depôts, produced the most beneficial effects. But as the Fund is now exhausted, they will, without fresh Contributions, be under the painful necessity of discontinuing these salutary supplies. To avert such a misfortune, they think it their duty to use every exertion in their power; and in thus recommending the New Subscription to your favor and protection, they hope they shall not be deemed guilty of any offensive intrusion.

The necessity for the Subscription is the more urgent, because France has rigorously prohibited the English Government from extending any Relief to the Prisoners; and it is therefore only by the Donations of Individuals that Relief can be applied: to the remitting of which the French Government make no objection.

For the former Subscription, considerable Sums were raised in some places through the influence of the Clergy, who considered the object deserving of recommendation in their Sermons, and the Committee would think it a great advantage to obtain the same valuable assistance now.

Very particular details of the distribution of the last Subscription have been received from France, and remain in the hands of the Secretary for inspection, who will be happy to furnish any further information that may be desired on the subject; and any Letters relating to the Prisoners, it is respectfully requested may be addressed to him under cover to FRANCIS FREELING, Esq. Post-Office.

I have the honor to remain,

Your obedient Servant,

Thos Ferguson

Secretary.

London: printed by W. Phillips, George-yard Lombard-street.

A letter from the Secretary of Lloyd's Patriotic Fund Committee announcing the need for a new subscription and inviting the clergy to recommend the Fund in their sermons. Whereas the French forbade help from the British Government, they did allow voluntary contributions to be sent for the relief of our prisoners of war.

their families. At the first forming the depôt the great circulation of money attracted from Paris many species of sharpers. A gambling Bank was licenced with every allurement attached to it which could draw the incautious youth into their intriguing snares. There were also various companies of comedians, and troops of performers from time to time causing a momentary change for the dissipated.

The Parole given by the *Gouvernement* was very liberal — that of three miles from the rampart in any direction, leaving with the guard at the gate at which one went out a passport or permit which was returned on our re-entry. The time of our going out was limited — sometimes from daylight till sunset — at other times from 8 a.m. till 4 p.m. The consequence of not returning at the appointed time — a fine of 2s/6d first offence. We were obliged to attend a muster of *appel* twice a day, between the hours of 8 and 10, and 2 and 4; but *détenus*, or officers of a superior rank were exempt from a daily call — they signed but twice a week. Missing *appel* was a fine of 2s/6d or prison — every little cause of complaint was fine, and very shameful were the instances of peculation practised by the General towards individuals; he even gave a small portion to the *gens d'armes* to encourage them to act with the utmost rigour.

In June 1805 two young gentlemen breaking their parole and several getting away by other means gave the general a plea to oblige the Captains to be responsible for the gentlemen of their respective ships; having no benefit of such protection, I was with many others conducted to the Citadel where we were confined to an old convent, having a yard in its centre of about sixty feet square for promenade — however but a few days elapsed when Captain Brenton, in his uniform kindness to me, brought Captain Gower to whom he introduced me and by whose application to Gen. Wirion I was again liberated. The year following both these benevolent protectors were exchanged, so that I became once more dependent on the capricious humour of the General — but in the hurry of business was not

A characteristic certificate from the Patriotic Fund accompanying the award of 50 pounds to the wounded Boatswain of the 32-gun frigate HMS *Cleopatra* after her action with a French frigate. The Chairman, John Julius Angerstein (1735–1823), had been an underwriter at Lloyd's since 1756. He was a great philanthropist, devised many state lotteries, and his collection of pictures, displayed at his home, 100 Pall Mall, was bought by the Government in 1824 and formed the nucleus of the National Gallery.

called on to provide a responsibility in lieu of Captain Gower. As our imprisonment lengthened so the number of desertions increased — some from a certain ruin of their affairs — and others in despair of an exchange. My friend Tuthill with four of our friends made up their minds to endeavour their escape and got safe out of Verdun: but to my unspeakable anguish they were discovered near Boulogne, and brought back in chains[24]. After suffering a rigorous confinement in the Citadel they were conducted to Bitche, a depôt where all deserters and *mauvais sujets* of every denomination were sent, and indiscriminately confined in subterranean cells.

Verdun was an ancient fortified town with a Citadel, and formerly the see of a Bishop, and contained some large well-built houses, and in consequence was well adapted for the reception of a large depôt. The Meuse, a large river, flowed through the town, and independent of the Ramparts there were some pleasant walks about the town. Every necessary of life was remarkably cheap, and *l'argent anglais* made all luxuries flow in, even the heads of Wild Boars from Westphalia. At the first formation of the depôt we had racing the first week of every month: this was fine amusement for the light-heeled Mids riding jockeys — in fact nothing was denied by the General that could be paid for — but money for everything. Amidst a great jumble of sharpers and people whose lives were devoted to the Turf, there were yet some very estimable characters, who endeavoured to restrain the youth and teach them the way in which they should walk. We were privileged to open a room formerly the chapel of a convent, which was fitted up for a church and Mr. Gorden[25], a very pious Minister, officiated. The Reverend Robert Wolfe was one whose devotion to the good of the sufferings of his fellow-prisoners deserves to be generally noted. He was detained at Fontainebleau, and sent to Verdun, who independent of his ministering to us each Lord's Day assisted by Mr. Gorden, opened a school for the boys taken in the vessels of war, and in the merchant vessels. These boys were clothed uniformly in neat Jackets and Trousers, through funds in Captain Brenton's hands, and marched to Church on the Sundays — but this caused much umbrage, and an order came from the Minister of War to

A pass issued by the Commandant at Verdun on 30 December 1812. This allowed an English prisoner of war, Lieutenant James Whitley, an infantry officer in the 9th Foot, to leave by certain gates on condition that he returned before they were closed. The permit contains a detailed description of his hair, face and height.

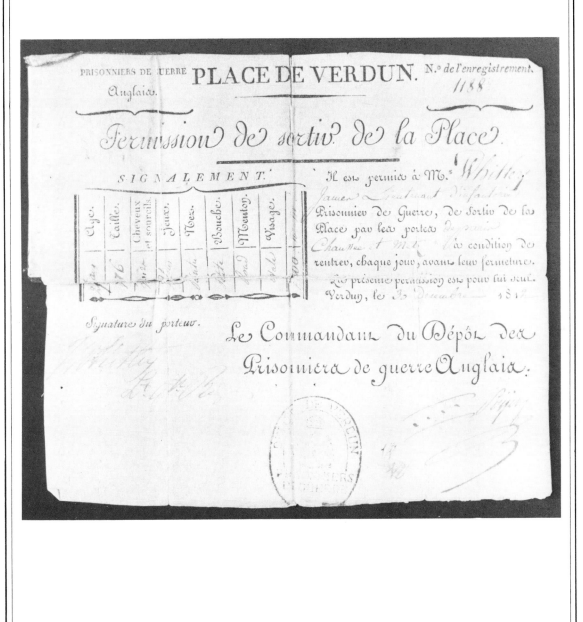

General Nicolas-Charles Oudinot (1767–1847) was created a Marshal after the battle of
Wagram in 1809 and became Duke of Reggio in the following year. Oudinot, who received
more than thirty wounds in Napoleon's service, first made his reputation as a battalion
Commander when fighting Prussian forces near Bitche and along the Meuse in 1792.

JOSÉPHINE ROSE TASCHER DE LA PAGERIE
BONAPARTE.

Femme du premier Consul

The Empress Joséphine (1763–1814), from a miniature by Isabey *c.* 1802. Born Marie Rose
Joséphine Tascher de la Pagerie, she married first the Vicomte de Beauharnais and had two
children, Eugène and Hortense. She was widowed in 1794, met General Bonaparte in the
following year and married him on 9 March 1796. She became Empress in 1804. The
marriage ended in divorce in 1809, and she spent the rest of her life at Malmaison.

The meeting of two Emperors at Tilsit on 25 June 1807. Napoleon
set off from the left bank of the Niemen accompanied by Marshals
Murat, Berthier and Bessières, and by Generals Duroc and
Caulaincourt. The Tsar Alexander left by boat from the opposite
bank with the Grand Duke Constantine, Generals Bennigsen and
Ouvarov, Prince Labonov and Count Lieven. The Emperors met on a
raft moored in midstream. The picture is from a drawing by Debret.

send them to Sarrelibre[26], a new depôt about then formed. This amiable gentleman hearing the depraved state of the English prisoners who were confined at Givet determined to sacrifice every personal comfort and alleviation in the society of many estimable friends, and devote himself to the reclaiming of men whom despair and suffering had almost rendered ferocious and desperate — but he had counted the cost, and though it involved personal danger, it was followed by such an amount of blessing as few have been permitted to witness. On his first removing to Givet he found the seamen sunk in every kind of abomination — half starved by the dishonesty of the French Commissaries, destitute of every comfort, and in a state of mind much to be pitied. The cruel and unfeeling policy of the French Government at the time led them to make the condition of the prisoners as wretched as possible, that they might be the more easily tempted by the Agents employed to reduce them from their allegiance, and the evils of captivity were studiously aggravated by the want of food and covering that the seamen might be induced to enlist in the French Service. A more fearful exhibition of human nature, it is hard to conceive, when Mr. Wolfe resolved to throw himself among them.

At the period of the war being declared with Austria[27], a large division of the Boulogne Army marched through Verdun, halting for the night, and nothing could exceed their fine appearance. Marchl. Oudinot marched in one day at the head of 10,000 grenadiers[28], a very fine body of men — tho' so crowded, the greatest order prevailed — not a man intoxicated. Buonaparte passed through twice on the occasion of his campaigns — the first time accompanied by Josephine[29], and on his return after the Treaty of Tilsit by Murat when he was received under triumphal Arches, and with great ceremony his favourite Mameluke at each time sitting on the driver's seat going through the Town — he attended by a guard of *gens d'armes* and a troop of young gentlemen. He breakfasted at the Inn, and went through at his leisure shewing himself to every one[30].

For some length of time I continued to live with Tuthill and Thorley. In 1805 seeing two young gentlemen strangers walking the streets looking for lodgings, I brought them home to partake of our dinner. They had just been marched up from Brest, and seemed very weary and overcome from fatigue. They belonged to the *Acasta* Frigate and had been made prisoners when going to the island of Béniquet for sand, having no sooner landed than they were surrounded by soldiers concealed in the cover. From their very severe treatment on the march — confined to *cachots*, and having no subsistence allowed them, I found them both ill the next morning in fever, on going to call them to breakfast. Mr. [Thomas George] Wills the Midshipman soon recovered, but Mr. McGraw remained a long time an invalid. When he recovered from the fever, rheumatic sores came out on him, and for nearly two years was confined to his bed in a most helpless state, and in such pain from his sores that he could suffer but me to go near him in his bed to move him on all occasions — and never did I devote myself to any person so earnestly, never thinking of leaving his room. At length change was recommended to him, and after lodging with us for something more than two years, he removed to my friend O'Brien: and about this time we also broke up house-keeping, each of us going to live *en pension*, that is, in French families for the purpose of learning French. I became an inmate of a Barber, but one who had much of the *manière* of the *Ancienne Noblesse*. His children were all very much advanced by the Revolution, but he was an honest upright man and soon became very much attached to me. Never shall I forget at the time of my confinement in the citadel, at the first peep of day, he would be at the gates watching to hear something of me, and when I was liberated, and came home, such was his joy that he burst into tears, and when I afterwards made my escape, my little dog became his companion, which he always kept at his side. With this honest family I was too happy. They did everything that depended on them to alleviate my imprisonment. I always occupied myself in study either in French or Italian: the evenings were spent walking with Mr Kitchen[31] (a young Scotch gentleman, taken going to India as a writer) on the ramparts, and in the winter evenings, we retired to his lodgings, where were invariably assembled a Mr. Melville-Innis and Mr. Burns. A cheerful fire and the politics of the day was our repast. Never were evenings more rationally spent, being all gentlemen who had seen much of the world, and whose vanities they had learned to contemn. Kitchen accompanied me every Sunday to church and in his religious and well-informed mind I found much to admire.

Napoleon Bonaparte in his coronation robes. He was crowned Emperor of the French in Notre-Dame in Paris on 2 December 1804. The drawing is by Isabey.

Grand Habit de sa Majesté l'Empereur Napoléon 1er
le jour du couronnement.

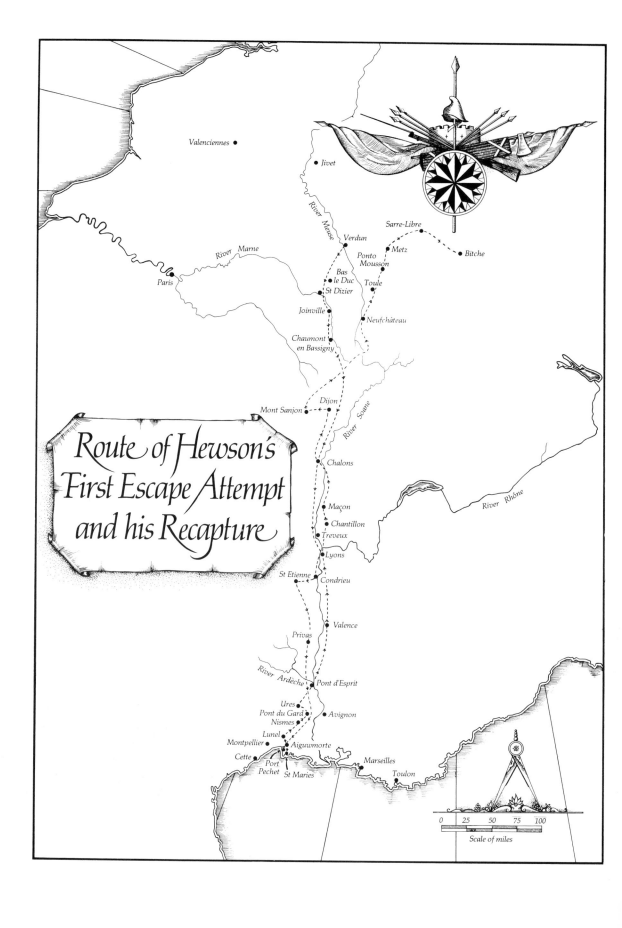

Route of Hewson's
First Escape Attempt
and his Recapture

Valenciennes

Jivet

River Meuse

River Marne

Sarre-Libre

Verdun

Metz

Ponto
Mousson

Bitche

Paris

Bas
le Duc

Toule

St Dizier

Joinville

Neufchâteau

Chaumont
en Bassigny

Mont Sanjon

Dijon

River Saône

Chalons

Maçon

River Rhône

Chantillon

Treveux

Lyons

St Etienne

Condrieu

Valence

Privas

River Ardèche

Pont d'Esprit

Ures

Pont du Gard

Avignon

Nismes

Lunel

Montpellier

Aiguwmorte

Cette

Marseilles

Port
Pechet

Toulon

St Maries

0   25   50   75   100

Scale of miles

III

The First Escape

THE year 1808 brought in very gloomy prospects for the poor prisoners
— the long continuance of confinement at Verdun and all hopes in an
exchange caused by the occasional openings between the two governments
now ceasing and the treaty of Tilsit closing every avenue for an indefinite
time. It required every energy of the mind to contend against the gloomy
prospect. By the removal of the greater number of my intimate friends —
some to Valenciennes — others to Bitche — I felt particularly depressed,
add to which the comfort of corresponding with our friends in England had
long been denied to us. I had now been nearly five years prisoner, losing
every knowledge I had gained of my profession, and still more, at my time
of life a burthen to my friends, without a chance of recommending myself
to my profession. Since Septr. 1806 I only enjoyed my enlargement from a
close confinement through the kind interference of Captain Gower. In
February 1808, I lost the passport, or permit, to go outside the town which
he got for me, without which I was denied that liberty, and on making
application for a second, it was denied me till I should find a substitute for
Captain Gower. Finding my correct conduct, since my coming to the depôt
had no avail, I immediately planned a scheme to effect my escape, for I
could no longer feel myself bound by any tie of parole. Soliciting another to
become answerable for me was of too delicate a nature: I therefore joined a
Mr. Butterfield[32] whom I found equally situated. We prepared some
necessaries, and conveyed them to a concealed place in a wood about three
miles from Town, without further hesitation to attempt to get back to my
country, my friends, and my profession, or suffer a closer imprisonment,
which on such an occasion had no terror.

'Twas on the night of the 13th March that we succeeded in getting over
the ramparts by means of a friend who lowered us by a rope unperceived by
the sentinels. We soon got to our rendez-vous in the wood, where we had
each a knapsack with provender for a fortnight, composed of crusts of
bread, sausages, and some spirits. We had maps of the Departments

through which we would have to pass, pocket-compass, and many little articles of no weight which we should need. For some time it was necessary to use the utmost precaution, for *gens d'armes* patrol the roads and path-ways immediately about Verdun: but as we distanced these detested walls we got on at a better rate, and began to feel more confidence. We were overcome with the thoughts of shaking off the load of such a cruel and oppressive confinement, yet grieved at parting from many worthy friends. We avoided every house and village, of which we had sufficient warning, on approaching, by dogs barking — and when alarmed by anything had recourse to a bush till all was quiet. When nearly about four leagues on our road, a small river stopped us, which we followed till we came to a Bridge — but, hearing a cart advancing towards us on the road, we got under one of its arches, till it should pass, when, to our surprise, on its approach it was challenged by a guard over-head: however while their attention was engaged by the *voiturier* we crept away as we came, and were for two hours tramping before we found a convenient place at which to cross the river. This delay prevented our reaching beyond Bar-le-Duc that night. At first dawn of day we retired to a wood where we concealed ourselves in a bushy part, but the whole was so thin of underwood, as to afford but indifferent shelter — but the place was lonesome. We then opened our sacks, and with hearts truly grateful to the Almighty who had thus far protected us, ate most heartily of this our first meal in liberty. So many people were passing and repassing the next day that we could scarcely venture to sleep — indeed our hearts were too much elated to admit of repose — sweet liberty too much possessed us. When night set in we rose from among our bushes and set forward. The night was very dark and cold and having unfortunately left our compass in a branch of a tree at our first starting, had now to trust to a view of the stars. At eleven we were stopped by a small river that I made an attempt to wade but it was too deep and too cold. I was so chilled that Butterfield obliged me to take a little spirits to revive me. We shortly after discovered a plank bridge leading across. We next entered a thick dreary wood where flights of wild ducks frequently started us. By following a small rivulet we at last reached Bas river [R. Ornain] at about two o'clock. Here we refreshed ourselves and meditated how to get across. Following its course we came to a bridge with the town of Bar-le-Duc on its opposite Bank. We had no alternative, but determined if we saw any guards, to retreat the same way. There were none; so easily overcoming this first dreaded difficulty enlivened us to march on with greater speed.

Before break of day we retreated to a nut wood as nearly as we could guess half way between Bar-le-Duc and St. Dizier — after our little meal and look to the Almighty in thanksgiving, we covered ourselves over with some dead leaves in a hole, and having great abundance of them made ourselves very comfortable, and for the first time ventured to nap, but short was our sleep. At daylight some guards coming through the wood, one of their dogs discovered us, and kept barking and rooting, till his master came to see what was the matter among the bushes. He asked with a smile if we were warming ourselves among the leaves, and then turned off to call some of the others to his assistance. As quick as thought we slipped on our sacks, pushed on under the bushes, in an opposite direction to the ditch of the wood in which there was a run of water leading under a road which being frozen very hard we concealed ourselves in the gullet till about noon, when conceiving that they had partly given over search, and more generally gone to dinner, we crossed the country as quickly as possible to a range of woods that we saw extending three or four miles, and again got to a close retreat. This was absolutely necessary, for the alarm of our *évasion* from Verdun would have run through the country the day before with description of our persons and a reward for our apprehension — so that all the guards and country people would have surrounded and searched the wood immediately with dogs.

This night we did not venture out till late — when after mutually imploring the protection of the Almighty and cordially shaking hands, a little habit we never omitted, as not knowing what the Lord might ordain for us the next moment, we were in the act of getting on the road from a stream of water at which we were drinking, which was our first want, and hearing the noise of horses approaching, lay down by its side. They were two *gens d'armes* returning with a man on foot, as we supposed from looking for us. About midnight we reached the banks of the Marne, which we followed in the direction of Joinville. We halted in a wood by the road side to refresh ourselves from the contents of our sacks, and having scarcely closed an eye since leaving Verdun, and overcome with fatigue we lay down to rest. We were instantaneously asleep. The piercing cold aroused us; nor until we walked some time did we recover our warmth. Towards morning we concealed ourselves on the rise of a high hill, and when the sun got a little warm, had its full benefit, and each in turn a good nap.

Thus did we get forward more or less every night as our strength would permit us, avoiding as much as possible the public roads, for the *gens d'armes* were in the habit of patrolling them. On the fourth night we crossed the Marne. The weather being very cold caused us to expend more of our spirits than we had calculated would have been necessary. Almost all the fifth day there was a fall of sleet and snow which prevented our getting any rest. We observed from our concealment a small Hut on the side of the road which from its lonely situation we determined to reconnoitre and if possible renew our provisions of brandy, &c. and when it became dark seeing but an old woman as its inmate, we ventured to ask for some supper. She fried some salt herrings for us, and procured for us some very bad white brandy, but we were compensated by getting some good bread. On leaving the Hut I was very much overcome by thirst. The salt herring and tasting the brandy, added to the effects of going near a large fire after such a long exposure to the open air, almost made me mad; nor for a length of time on the road could I get anything but snow, which made me worse: at last, coming up a hill, Butterfield got me some water — but thirst never so overcame me before. This night we passed Chaumont en Bassigny, the place at which I had been so long confined to the Hospital. How different were now my thoughts and hopes from that morning when I left it on a car for Verdun. The Lord was graciously pleased to spare me. He who delights not in the death of a sinner restored me to a return of health, which I believed I should never enjoy, & caused me to look forward with hopes to better times, though I had but indifferent health at Verdun: and even on the eve of coming away, in talking to a friend of the number of *évasions* from the depôt, his saying was, 'that if he was too corpulent, I was far too delicate for such an undertaking, being attended with great fatigue and hardship' — but from the moment I left its hated walls it seemed to me that I recovered strength and health beyond my expectation. The change of diet and being so long under the open element occasioned a short sickness, but my friend Butterfield felt it more severely, though of very strong consitution. In the morning it came on a very thick fog — we could neither make out our route, nor a place in which to conceal ourselves — but stumbled unawares on a village: about ten it cleared away, and we found ourselves in the middle of a large field where several people were at work sewing grain, but they took no notice of us. We soon got to a wood and calculated on being now about Eighty miles from Verdun which much cheered us.

The further we advanced in our journey, the more confidence we assumed in procuring bread and sometimes a bottle of wine, always keeping up a reserve in our provision: but caution was the order of the day. Whenever we approached a lonely house at night we first looked about it, and if possible in at the windows, and had a retreat in view the moment day would appear — a wood was our first search to conceal ourselves in close ambush. The weather from time to time was much against us — frequently it rained the entire day, which was a preventive to our sleeping, except by our collecting stones and forming a bed of them, and such was our wearied state that we soon got accustomed to it. Poor Butterfield's shoes were so heavy they chafed and ulcerated his feet very much, and the road being wet and muddy (for now being distant from Verdun we ventured on the roads) and from the nights being dark unable to see his steps, he walked in most excruciating pain. My feet were blistered in a slight degree, but nothing to equal my poor friend's — but the cheering hopes of getting to our country banished from our thoughts all difficulties.

Many and various were the crosses we sustained, but we seldom felt want of provision, suiting our daily allowance to the weight of our sacks, taking occasional opportunities of refurnishing them, and in lieu of spirits procuring wine. We found no risk in passing through the small villages but never ventured near a Town.

On the fourteenth day we reached Lyons (or rather its neighborhood) which was 270 miles from Verdun. The Lord had been wonderfully merciful to us in conducting us thus safely through a country, which was at each moment beset with difficulties and hair-breadth escapes too monotonous to mention. We wished to cross the Bridge but seeing a sentinel, we returned and had a long march round to get at the suburbs. In the morning, on looking for a place in which to conceal ourselves, we met a milk-woman going with her milk to Lyons, of which we each drank most heartily: and by some questions finding that she had but her little child at home, her husband having gone to work in some direction, we induced her return to her home by buying from her the remainder of her can, which she boiled for us with some bread: and then shewing us to an out-house where there was some straw, we slept there till about noon, when she had a piece of salt Pork boiled for us. We stored our sacks with whatever her house could afford us — then, handsomely repaying the poor woman, crept to the shades of a wood, like the evil Demons of Night.

For two or three days we kept a direction leading us parallel to the Rhône through the mountains that we might get a little distance from Lyons before venturing to descend on the road leading along its bank, which we intended to follow. The mountain air was so cold we were frequently obliged to quit our retreat earlier than prudence would dictate. The first evening of our approaching the river, being out earlier than usual we passed a *gen d'armes* crossing a small bridge by whom it was our good fate not to be questioned.

Every night we met as we passed near any houses (which were on this line

La Laitiere?

for the most part *Traiteurs* or drinking houses) numbers of sailors who were always very inquisitive, & we were two or three times put to the flight by *Douaniers* or Custom-House Officers who were stationed in great numbers along the river. Finding our line of road too dangerous to be persevered in, we again took to the mountain districts, keeping a centre route from Condrieux to Privas and St. Etienne. We suffered great hardships in this part of our journey, as well from the difficulty of making out our road, as from our hair-breadth escapes of discovery, which we owed much to the exercise of our wit, or some unexpected chance — for the inhabitants of the mountains being unaccustomed to strangers, and the cold forcing us from our nests before dark we could not avoid being perceived by more people than we could have wished, and to whom we caused much suspicion.

Though apparently going along as if passing through a gauntlet, how singular it was that we enjoyed the greatest spirits, every difficulty or disentanglement only giving cause to joke on the occasion. One night having just passed St. Etienne, while it was blowing and raining very hard, passing near a Farm-house, we made free by entering an out-office for shelter from the weather for a short time: there were some mules staked up, from whom we took a little supernumerary straw, first securing the door against surprise. When just in the full comforts of a nap, the Muleteer came thumping at the door, which finding in some strange way to be fastened occasioned from him a few round oaths and from us no little trepidation — however gently removing the cause of his wrath without his suspecting the inmates, he took his accustomed berth at the head of his *dapples*, when soon after we skulked off, well securing the door on the outside.

Very often not finding cover to conceal ourselves among the arid mountains of Ardèche we would seek some quarry or lonely concealed spot, and, when our meal and morning nap over, we would amuse ourselves with tales of our youth, and looking at the passing scene below us, always finding something with which to amuse ourselves, but never forgetting our great and merciful Protector, and commending ourselves to his gracious care. On passing Privas a man coming out of a house which we had just passed joined us in conversation, and became by his inquisitiveness

A French milk-woman. After their escape from Verdun Hewson and Butterfield were helped by a milk-woman outside Lyons.

very troublesome — at last, in the name of the law, commanding us to stop, and shew our passports, & calling on two men who were walking after us to come to his assistance. This was too much: I tripped him gently on the road, and before he recovered was some distance off. We at last reached the banks of the Ardèche River. Our map gave us but one bridge upon it which was at some distance from us, and quite at right angles with our route: therefore not to lose time we determined to swim across. I undertook to go first with my clothes tied in a bundle over my neck — then returned for provisions and last of all to accompany Butterfield and bring across his sack. When I landed I was very weak from being in the water so long, and for a time lost all sense of my situation with a giddiness in my head. Butterfield seeing my situation assisted me in getting on my clothes, and made me drink some wine. I then crawled with him to a house, and though we offered two *Louis* to be allowed in to warm ourselves, they refused admittance, but discovering the Pig-sty adjoining we soon took their places. At first a shivering overcame me. At last recovering almost in a benumbed state, gathered up my sack, &c. and ran on the road as fast as I could till I got warm and recovered.

The next night in travelling along our road, we met an *auberge* and, in pretence of getting bread, called for some supper: but they detained us so long preparing it that we were obliged to call for beds lest our going away at that late hour might cause suspicion. Under excuse of business requiring us early at Nîmes we had the key left in the door, and when we believed all in the house in the enjoyment of sleep dressed ourselves — and crept quietly away, and proceeded again *en route*. When two miles on I found that I had forgotten my watch on the pillow: so leaving my sack with Butterfield, ran back and got into the room again, and safe out, without being heard. The following night we passed Nîmes: when it came morning, we were for some time seeking a hiding-place, and were at last obliged to get into a rick of dryed faggots, which are piled up like ricks of hay. Being well sheltered from observation we gave vent to the pleasing hope of approaching the end of our long journey, and were enjoying a peculiar flow of spirits — when about four in the evening a large cart drew near us and on it some women and children, who to our great consternation began to load the cart with

A *douanier* or custom house officer. In 1814 an English traveller to Paris, Dr William Roots, described the *douaniers* in Calais as 'a surly-looking, half-soldierly people, wearing a dark green uniform and an immense great cocked hat'.

our covering till they fairly discovered us when they ran off as if quite frightened to some little distance, and allowed us to move off without notice — but again the *maudite* watch was forgotten, and on returning for it, they allowed me to take it, running away from the rick as before, such was the simplicity of these poor *paysans* at seeing strangers. It was impossible for us to find another place to conceal ourselves — there being no woods to be seen — and we were observed by the country people around working in the fields. We followed a pathway which led us to a Farm-house, where they gave us some bread and milk. They seemed particularly anxious to know where we were going to. I said to Marseilles to seek some employment. They would not suffer us to pay for our bread and milk. Our next adventure was in crossing a canal leading to Aigues-Mortes at a Fisherman's Hut where they were very civil to us and told us what vessels were ready for sailing. About 11 o'clock we reached this first seaport town to which vessels could come up by a canal four miles long.

It would be difficult for me to give an adequate idea of our feelings and gratitude to Divine Providence in having protected us in so long and arduous an undertaking. This was the fourteenth of April, the thirtieth day since our leaving Verdun, without our having slept, but once under cover and subsisting on bread of which at times we had very short allowance, and frequently only water to drink with it. Two or three times we got a little pork and hard-boiled eggs. And this at a season when the trees having no leaves afforded us little shelter. On recollection of the many difficulties we had to overcome, I am astonished how we overcame them, and with what light hearts we treated the thought of them. We had many hair-breadth escapes of being arrested, which it would have been too tedious to relate, but which inspired us with confidence and a presence of mind which the occasions demanded.

We did not go into Aigues-Mortes till after 12 o'clock, when we found from what we learned from a man who told us that he belonged to the *Douane*, that we met in the street that we could do nothing from thence, the vessels were so strictly examined. We then took the road towards Fort Pechet a more advanced situation but found too many soldiers and *Douaniers* in this station. We crossed the Rhône at Pechet and went to Les Saintes Maries which we passed through at an early hour the next night that we might see its harbour. We were questioned by two of the guards, and for some time conversed with them. Towards morning we returned to the town most cautiously, but guards were stationed in too many places around it, so watchful that we dare not approach near enough to observe where any Boats were lying. On our retreat we found a thicket of rushes near the Beach where we concealed ourselves, and two or three times, after day light, popped up our heads to see what was passing. In the afternoon a convey of vessels, thirty in number, passed us going to Sète; and when it became dark we went on the beach to some boats which were hauled up seemingly rotting without masts or sails. We again ventured into Saintes Maries and much to our disappointment found there were no masted boats in the place, and to venture without a sail to sea, with our provisions only six pounds of bread, a bottle of water, and one of wine, would have been the utmost rashness; for Sardinia which was our nearest place of safety was 180 miles from us; so with sad hearts were obliged to resign a hope which had till now buoyed us up. Our prospects of success were no longer so sanguine: we looked too much to our own strength and not to that of the Lord. There was no place on this extreme point of the mouth of the Rhône where we could venture to seek for provisions, so were forced to retreat before they were exhausted.

At about four in the morning we re-crossed the Rhône in a Boat and seeing the place most lonely asked the old man for something for breakfast, under pretence of having left Saintes Maries too early for getting anything to eat. On entering his hut we were struck with surprise to behold two *gens d'armes* dressing themselves as if preparing to arrest us. I collected all my presence of mind, and after freely saluting them, entered on my own story — that we came the evening before from Marseilles, and landed at Saintes Maries — that we intended going to Montpellier by way of Lunel; this tale told with a good deal of *sangfroid* had the desired effect, for Lunel was a Town where a strong Brigade of *gens d'armes* were stationed and where they knew we dare not venture without being perfectly *en règle*. We induced them to take part of our *déjeûner* with us, and after a little indifferent chit-chat they came with us a little distance to shew us the nearest road. We were not a little pleased with ourselves in getting so well over this little embarrassment. At the next house at which we stopped, we were told that these men had been sent there to arrest two young Spaniards, who it was supposed were endeavouring to get to Italy, whom we suspected to be none others than ourselves: for at the farmer's house at which we stopped, before going to Aigues-Mortes they hinted at our being two *pauvres Espagnols*.

The swamps and salt water tanks for making salt from evaporation were so spread over this district of the country that we were forced to walk in open day to extricate ourselves from them — for it was all cut thro' by channels conveying the salt water to the highest level. The salt in France yields a great revenue, and in order to prevent smuggling there were numerous stations where *Douaniers* and *gardes-Côtes* were stationed. Thus we had a most anxious day's march getting by the several guards, who challenged us in passing, demanding our route, &c. Our morning's story was our general answer. At dusk we were passing a Fisherman's hut whose inmates came out to meet us, enquiring if we were from Toulon — the proprietor told us that two of his sons were just arrived there from Rochefort, whom he expected soon to see come home to him. They gave us some bread and wine. We were suspected by them to be two conscripts deserting from the ships, and wished us most heartily good luck in reaching our homes.

Not far from the fisherman's we had to pass a guard house, where an officer of the *Douane* was stationed. He stopped us to examine our passports. I told him that the previous morning we embarked in a small vessel at Marseilles with the intention of going to Sète, but a storm coming on that both my companion and myself entreated the captain to land us, who acceding to our urgent prayer put us into a fishing-boat passing by to whom we had to pay six *livres*, but when we approached near the shore which the Boat struck I was so frightened that in getting out too hastily I fell into the water, and lost out of my pocket my pocket-book, in the sea, together with two Crown pieces and my Knife — that our passports and some letters of recommendation from our friends at Marseilles to people at Montpellier were in my pocket-book. For some time he kept us in conversation. I answered his questions with the greatest air of simplicity — at last telling us that the road to Montpellier was so beset by *gens d'armes* that without a *carte de sûreté*, we should be stopped, and recommended our going to the Mayor of Aigues-Mortes, who was a very good man and who would furnish us with one that would protect us. This held out such a hope to us that I too credulously grasped at anything like getting the name of a person in authority, and begged the Lieutenant to give us a note to him: but

Above: Aigues-Mortes: the northern ramparts, showing from right to left the Porte de la Gardette, the Tour du Sel, the Porte Saint-Antoine, the Tour de la Mèche, and the Tour de Villeneuve. The painting was made some time before 1835.

Below: The Tour de Constance, which served as a lighthouse for centuries, and the western walls of Aigues-Mortes. The illustration dates from soon after 1800.

he said he was not known to the Mayor — his Captain was at the next post, and he was sure that he would write to him for us, and sent a man to shew us the way to his post. The Captain gave such credit to the report of his Lieutenant that he never questioned us, but went to his bureau to further his request, inviting us to sit down and partake of a very nice supper at which he had been seated with his wife. At this moment a most inquisitive person entered who at once questioned Butterfield on the manner of making hats, which was the trade which he assumed. From his not speaking good French I told him that he was a Swiss lad who came to Marseilles to learn his trade not much more than twelve months. This caused him to be more troublesome, so much so that he influenced the Captain to change his opinion of us — he tore the note he had written and now sent us as two strangers found on his station without passports; and in a short time after we were placed in a boat and sent up to Aigues-Mortes by canal. I feigned being very sick from the motion of the boat, and at each moment stretched myself over the gunnel to throw my maps and papers into the water, which the darkness of the night favoured: and then lying down in the bottom of the boat groped from Butterfield's pockets those which he had about him wishing them all a speedy passage to the bottom — still feigning sickness.

At one o'clock we reached Aigues-Mortes and were placed in the prison of the guard-house, and in the morning the Secretary of the Commandant came to examine us as to the report made by the Captain. We still maintained the same story, and most piteously begged him to intercede for us with the Mayor — with every power of utterance and humility praying that we might not suffer detention from so innocent a cause, which would materially injure us at Montpellier: but this gentleman was not to be moved by our entreaties — the suffering of a fellow-creature had no part in his nature — he decided by saying that he believed us to be *deux sacrés conscrits*.

I sincerely trust that the dilemma we were thown into may palliate the inventive fable which we had prepared to carry out our design. Our case was most desperate, and to succeed required a forethought and presence of mind continually on the alert. We had now been for three or four days without taking rest, and were greatly overcome. Our next visitor was the old Commandant whose countenance at once spoke something more flexible than those we had previously met. His first questions were aimed at knowing when we had drawn for Conscripts. I told him that I had *réformé*, that is found a substitute about three years before — that my Commune was Dijon, *du* Côte d'or[33] — that I was the son of a Barber, who resided in

A view of Aigues-Mortes from the eastern ramparts from an early nineteenth-century painting. The Tour de Constance can be seen in the distance.

Rue Chausiron *près* la porte de Paris in a small shop. He told me that his parents lived at Dijon. On learning his name I pretended to have heard my old father speak of him with great respect and entirely to his generous feeling was he indebted for his small *Boutique*, for he had been greatly broken down by the times. He questioned Butterfield to the same effect, who told him that he was a Swiss from the Canton de Vaud, and that he came to Marseilles to be bound to a hat-maker who was related to his mother — that we had been living near each other and formed a mutual friendship, and as long as we could conveniently get work in the same town, we should not separate. This good man seemed to be much interested for us, and promised me all the assistance in his power. Some others came to see us from motives of curiosity. At noon we were conducted under a guard to the Municipality where the Mayor and chief authorities of the Town were assembled. I was perfectly calm and collected during their examination of me, committing myself to the care of Him who looks down on all his creatures. A *Procès-verbal* was drawn out of the particulars of my losing my passports. They required the name of the Captain in whose vessel we embarked at Marseilles — his landing us but at our destined Port was contrary to law — this I said was caused by his seeing me so very ill, and that he did not think I could survive it, and referred the gentlemen to the Boatmen who brought us to Aigues-Mortes, and pleaded a voluntary surrender of myself: but the Mayor said that he must detain us, until he could write to Marseilles to know the truth of my statements, and recommended me writing to my old master, which would much facilitate my getting away; but I said he would only rejoice in my distress, as he was not at all pleased at my leaving him. Butterfield was now examined, but I was soon recalled to explain some of his answers — for he could not speak French sufficiently distinctly to be understood.

When we reflected on the small chance that remained to us of succeeding in the glimmering hope of getting passports to Montpellier, and that concealing longer our real character was only prolonging our sufferings, we each of us were much enfeebled in our health, as well from the alternate wants of food, drink, and rest — the long marches at night, animated with the hope of liberty, had much exhausted our strength — our funds were also much lowered, at least, too much to permit us in prudence to look forward to seek success in an undertaking such as the first for some time.

With Butterfield's leave, and with a heavy heart, I therefore made known unto them our little imposition, as a *dernier ruse de guerre*: but we had now much trouble to convince them of our real characters, particularly the

96

Commandant who was about to use his influence with the Mayor from (as he supposed) my being his countryman, and was at first very angry with me; when assured of our being English, he ordered the guards to be doubled, reminding them that they had not boys to deal with. I cannot but with pleasure mention the sympathy and commiseration felt for our long imprisonment, and fatigues, and hardships, almost expressing sorrow at our being arrested, saying such a confinement sanctioned any attempt at escape. The Mayor ordered a dinner for us, and everything was done to relieve our sufferings, and I really believe that many were sorry for our capture. In the evening we were re-conducted to the guard-house and the following morning (Monday) were conducted to Lunel, under an escort of twelve men with strong instructions to the *sergent* to be cautious of us — and here a ridiculous scene occurred in coming to a river, which we had to pass in a ferry-boat not large enough to contain us and our twelve soldiers: after much consultation part of the guard was passed over first — we were then sent with a second division, and the whole was passed over.

At about 12 o'clock we reached Lunel and were given over to the goading chains of the *gens d'armes* and marched same afternoon to Nîmes in handcuffs, and confined in the prison in the Citadel, which contained a great number of prisoners of all classes, and being situated on a height promised to be very healthy. There being every probability of a long detention in this place, we hired a room to ourselves for a *livre* a day, which gave us some consideration in the eyes of its motley inmates. On the second day we wrote to the *Préfet*, stating the motives of our *évasion* from Verdun, and as prisoners of war entreated that generous consideration for which his country was so justly distinguished — we claimed his protection and entreated a subsistence suitable to our rank in our service. His answer was that of a gentleman — couched in the mildest terms — inviting us to make known to him what had been allowed us at Verdun, which he would do all in his power to have remitted to us, and though our *évasion* was contrary to law, yet he would neglect nothing to mitigate its rigour. In a second letter we thanked him warmly for having so humanely interested himself to alleviate our misfortunes, and told him that we had been allowed 28 francs monthly. In a few days after he came to inspect the prison, and on his requiring to see us repeated his assurance in most affable terms that our subsistence would be remitted to us, and in the meantime endeavoured to reconcile us to our situation, and to make ourselves as comfortable as circumstances would permit.

A Mr. Cuppaidge, an Irish gentleman living at Nîmes on his parole, came

Paul Gregoire Journ et mout 1786

Nîmes: a drawing by Paul Oregani dated 1786. On the left is part of the Roman amphitheatre, known as Les Arènes. To the right stands the Maison Carrée, built in the first century BC. It has served as town hall, private residence, stable and church.

to see us by the desire of the *Préfet*. He was most attentive to us, and ordered his *Traiteur* to bring us in daily our dinner, for which we paid but ten pence. It came in under covers, and a cloth overcovering all, on a tray: thus enjoying a regular meal, and rest, together with the wholesome air of the Citadel soon restored us from our debilitated state of health, and we both returned to our usual buoyancy of spirits. There was hardly a day that large parties of refractory conscripts were not brought in and out by the *gens d'armes*. It is strange to the mind of an Englishman, that soldiers thus dragged in chains to their respective regiments should leave but few places from the Mediterranean to the Narva[34] unconquered: not in defending their own country, but to glut the insatiable ambition of a self-willed tyrant: but such is the grovelling spirit of this once great and high-minded nation, that all spirits are now subdued to the one mandate.

We always found something new to beguile the time among the motley crew that surrounded us. Among the class of civil prisoners many appeared to us more unfortunate than culpable, and many told us that they had been in decent circumstances in their position in society, but reduced from untoward causes.

As we had taken a room from the garden it gave a freedom in the prison, confined to that class alone. There was a large yard for prisoners to walk in. A portion of the day the men were locked up, and females were permitted to come down. Two decent women were of that order that they had at all times liberty, and located a room near us. They had failed in trade, but were supported and visited by their friends in town, and possessed mind to feel for, and endeavoured to relieve to the utmost of their power the very great misery before them — characters rarely to be met with in such places — and when any strangers came to see them from town, *Messieurs les Anglais* were sure to be introduced, and in partaking of the smile which their conviviality cast on all, we oft-times were led to forget our troubles. *Les Français ne portent jamais les idées noires.*

In this manner nearly two months elapsed without hearing from the *Préfet* if any sum was to be paid us by the Commissary of War for our subsistence: which induced us to write to him to say, that in the confidence of his generous assurance of a subsistence being granted to us, we had expended what remained to us of our small funds, to procure the most moderate food, and unless relieved by his promised bounty, would be reduced to prison allowance, consisting of a pound of bread only, that if no order as yet came for our removal to a depôt, we would earnestly entreat him to direct the Commissary of War to make us some remittance, which he was generous enough to say should be remitted to us. In the course of the week he favoured us with an answer, saying that he was directed by the Minister of War to give us over to the Genl. of Division commanding the district, who was ordered to send us under escort to Bitche — and in answer to our request for subsistence said that none was allowed to prisoners out of their depôts. Being foiled in this hope, we had no resource but what we might anticipate through Mr. Cuppaidge, who was generous enough to supply us with four *louis*, the which, with five that yet remained to us, formed our provision for another campaign.

A drawing by Genillion of the Pont du Gard from the Nîmes road. It
formed part of the Roman aqueduct which brought water to Nîmes
from near Uzès. The upper level of the bridge has thirty-five arches
and is 300 yards long. Hewson and Butterfield crossed under an
escort of *gendarmes* in June 1808.

IV

The Fortress of Bitche

ON the 6th June we recommenced our march under the escort of the *gens d'armes*, and were chained to some poor conscripts going the same road — the chain was passed round the neck with a small padlock attaching it which at times was squeezed tight, and which in warm days scalded the neck from the friction. During our long detention at Nîmes we experienced so many civilities and such general attention that we could not but feel sorry at leaving them. Some of the poor creatures came offering us their loaves of bread — others a few sous — and one of the old ladies before alluded to brought us some sausages sent to her by her daughter the previous day — in short all seemed to feel with the utmost consideration for us, and still more so, on seeing the *gens d'armes* chaining us.

At four o'clock we reached Uzès having crossed the Pont du Gard so much noticed as being a work of extraordinary minds — building a bridge of one arch span reaching from cliff to cliff, far above the water, and built of never-ending materials, far above our idea of architecture. The Brigadier of the party conducting us having mentioned to me that the Mayor of Uzès had a son long confined in the prisons in England, I told him that perhaps I might relieve his anxiety for his son. We were not long arrived before *Madame la Mairesse* paid me a visit accompanied by her daughter. With all the anxiety and tender feeling of a mother's heart, she came to know if I could give her any tidings of her son, who had been serving on board the *Mont Blanc* at the Battle of Trafalgar: but when she last heard from him he had been confined at Plymouth in the *Bienfaisant* Hulk. Butterfield who had been at Plymouth long after my capture was enabled to give her some comfort as to the general mild treatment shewn to the prisoners of war in England. The following morning the Mayor came to us to the intent and with an offer to serve us in any way in his power. He told us that a Society existed among the Protestants in Uzès who had a fund for mutual support of which he was president, and most generously offered to assist us, but we declined accepting anything from motives of delicacy. We gave him the

103

Prison hulks at Portsmouth, from the painting by Louis Garneray. About one third of the French prisoners of war held in this country — in 1811 the total was around 49,000 — were kept aboard hulks at Chatham and Plymouth as well as at Portsmouth. These hulks were dismantled ships, worn out and unfit for sea service, converted into floating prisons: overcrowded, very uncomfortable, damp and rotting. Use of hulks was intended as a

temporary measure until more prisons had been built on land such as Dartmoor and Perth, but there were always more prisoners of war than prisons in which to accommodate them.

Garneray, who served in the French navy, was captured by the British in 1806, and spent the next eight years at Portsmouth as a prisoner of war. One of his two volumes of memoirs, *Mes Pontons* (1861), describes his experiences on board a prison hulk.

names of people through whom he might correspond with his son, or remit him any money he pleased — at the same time taking charge of a letter for him which we forwarded from Bitche.

An interesting scene occurred when the Brigadier of *gens d'armes* came to chain us for our march in his asking me to tell him not to put such degrading humility on me by handcuffing us — such was his high estimation of the word of an Englishman; that he would be satisfied with the smallest assurance that we would not attempt our escape from him — and we found in many places very lenient treatment from the *gens d'armes* — though at times the very reverse actuated them. At the correspondence where we always exchanged guards, or rather at some little distance before we reached it, our chains were taken off, and the Brigadier told us that we would not again be chained, and in consequence of his speaking to the Brigadier of the relieving guard they were not resumed.

On the road to Avignon where we halted for the night we crossed the Pont St. Esprit, another bridge built by the Romans over the Rhône, and were confined to the Military gaols, and allowed, as on my march from Brest to Verdun, but a small allowance of bread, and the usual prison straw. On going to Valence we saw the hills of Ardèche, where in our route down we concealed ourselves frequently, on the opposite side of the Rhône. We often thought that we observed the very nooks in the stupendous mountains we crossed where we concealed ourselves from the passing eye, regarding the things below us as another creeping world most diminutive in size.

Our road from Valence was next towards Lyons: the weather was oppressively hot on the marches, and being chained to twenty or thirty in a row caused the marching to be indeed most fatiguing. The prisoners were generally permitted to breakfast where the *gens d'armes* exchanged correspondence which was about noon — many had but their loaf of brown bread while others would indulge in a Bottle of Wine which cost but three half-pence. We generally tried to get something more substantial — and in the *cachots* where they could supply us with beds, *Messieurs les Anglais* were sure to be first served.

In this route I never suffered anything like the treatment which I experienced going from Brest to Verdun and in Butterfield's sober mind I felt the consoling comfort of a dear friend. We mutually derided every little act of petulancy as coming from a mean source in those who were conducting us, & suffered them not to fret us. A companion with whom I could thus commune was an invaluable treasure sincerely felt — and having a little money to meet our wants made our fatigues comparatively a pleasure. There was certainly one instance of overbearing wantonness which overcame us — 'twas on our day's march to Lyons. At the stations of the correspondence when the Brigadier changes prisoners they also change handcuffs — each Brigadier having his own chains and padlocks, with which they always come provided. After our repast, *comme à l'ordinaire*, when chaining us for the road a poor Piedmontois who was covered with sores and vermin had been rejected by all the sons of the great nation to have placed near to them. The Brigadier observed aloud that there were *deux sacrés Anglais par là auxquels il l'enchaînerait*. I should have said nothing to this but he accompanied the action with much scurrilous language accusing our country as the cause of these poor conscripts being thus led along in chains — which called forth an indignant reply. This poor man from his pains and enfeebled body could not march but with difficulty and was an object to call forth the compassion of the most obdurate — and as he could not keep pace with the horses, the Brigadier drew his sword with the intention of striking me, calling on me to drag him along — but I looked on him with the most sovereign contempt, and gave him as much of the chain as I could afford so as to allow him to pick his steps.

At about four o'clock we reached Lyons very much overcome from the excessive sultry heat of the day, and we had marched 28 miles. When the gates were opened we were led into a large Portico with benches on which some sat down who could get seats. Owing to the pressure from the large number of prisoners coming in, the Turnkey had some difficulty in taking the padlocks off the chains, he vociferated many oaths, and Butterfield being next him, dragged him by the chain in a cruel manner — which from the friction of the handcuffs in the burning sun made his wrists very sore, and which he felt most acutely, and resented in a firm tone, but milder than the wretch merited, for which he was instantly unchained, & conducted to one of the *cachots* of the prison. I endeavoured to make some excuse for him, but for attempting to plead his cause was confined to a second dungeon, though I entreated not to be separated from my companion. I tried to procure pen and ink to make known such treatment as well to the *Préfet* as to the Military Commandant, but to no purpose — nor during our

Overleaf: The city of Lyons, showing the bridge across the Rhône. Hewson and Butterfield were confined in separate and filthy dungeons, and the gaoler and his turnkeys insulted them roundly for being English.

stay in this place would they allow us to purchase any sustenance more than our bread which was the prison allowance — a thing never previously denied to us. The dungeon in which I was confined was large enough to accommodate four people. Some dirty straw stood in one corner which I suspected to be full of vermin, so sat down on my knapsack at the most respectable distance permitted by the walls of my apartment — not so my fellow-inmates, for I had not been long left in cogitation over the occurrences of the day, when I observed myriads of fleas as if seeking to burrow through the pores of my trousers most obstinately determined to draw from me what I could then but little spare to them. Seeing myself surrounded by such a host, I determined upon leaving them my *overhauls*, as well as the field of battle, and retreating to a small window somewhat resembling a loop hole on one side of the cell, where I hoped they would no longer torment me, I sat for the remainder of the evening, much amused, building castles in the air. At about 8 o'clock the gaoler and two of his Turnkeys came their rounds; they addressed me in a most abusive tone for being an Englishman; not being able to move my silent contempt, the gaoler seized me by the collar and flung me with all his force on the dirty straw which lay in a heap in the corner, saying 'Va-t-en, foutu canaille Anglais, couche-toi sur la paille'.

We now from Lyons entered on the road over which we had passed with buoyant hearts full of hope and free as air on our route to the south, but now chained and handcuffed driven before two horsemen, as culprits accused of the deepest crime. We were, however, far from being dejected — the passing circumstances only so far affected us, as they fatigued the body. Our thoughts were still bent on escape, and the beautiful scenery of the country on our daily marches much enchanted us — thus the weighty chain and its degradation found its antidote; but I must say that some few of the *gens d'armes* took off our chains and Hand-cuffs at the correspondence. In the prisons, having a small command of money, gave us some little consideration in the eyes of the wives of the gaolers, who, of all people I ever met, were the most covetous class. We had tolerably clean beds and

Above: A view, by Lallemand, of Mâcon and the River Saône, spanned by the fourteenth-century Pont St Laurent. The tower marked by two birds overhead belongs to the Church of St Pierre.

Below: Dijon: the Palace of the Dukes of Burgundy, with the Chambre des Comptes on the left. The drawing is by Lallemand.

roughed it much better than on the route from Brest: than which nothing could be more degrading or loathsome.

On the road to Trévoux the views on the banks of the Saône were very beautiful. We halted for the night at Chatillon, where we were kindly treated being allowed the full liberty of the gaol: having halted here for a couple of days, we washed our shirts, and repaired our thin, worn garments. We next proceeded to Mâcon, about fifteen leagues from Lyons. I thought here of writing to the general commanding the troops at Lyons to complain to him of the ill treatment which we endured from the gaoler of that place, but we were so ill-natured as to wish that he might be long continued to rule over the prisoners, and that getting him removed would be doing an act of kindness to themselves. Mâcon is a Departmental Town, and beautifully situated on the Banks of the Saône. We proceeded next to Châlons passing through the heart of the rich wine country — each hill covered with vines. We halted a few days at Dijon, a large Town formerly a place of great note. This was the town I told the good Commandant at Aigues-Mortes I resided at. We were now about 33 leagues from Lyons. The weather was very hot, but we did not suffer much from it, being now enured to marching at all times. Leaving Dijon our road now branched off from the one leading to Paris, taking the road that leads to Metz by Montsaugeon, Nogent and Neufchâteau, Toul and Pont à Mousson. Arrived at Metz we felt as if drawing close to our own countrymen, and our own quarters. All English prisoners transmitted from Verdun to Sarre-Louis or Bitche were always halted here. It was now about the middle of July. We had previously written to our friends in Verdun, announcing to them our capture and the failure of all our hopes, and saying that we anticipated passing about this time *en route* to Bitche. The Prison of Metz was a very large establishment: it was but one day's march from Verdun. The day after my arrival I was much surprised by a visit from the daughter of my landlord, who was married to a Mons. Martin, a Captain in the Engineers, who had much distinguished himself. I had known her at

Metz: women doing their laundry in the Moselle. Behind rises the Cathedral of St Etienne. After their recapture, Hewson and Butterfield stopped in Metz on their way to confinement in the fortress of Bitche.

The drawing is by Samuel Prout (1783–1852), the watercolour painter who made his name with a series of continental street scenes begun in 1818.

Verdun. She came there once or twice to visit her father. It distressed me much seeing her come to such a shocking place accompanied alone by her sister-in-law. The change in my appearance seemed to distress her very much, and her generous sympathy in my misfortunes I shall never forget. She believed I had suffered very severely, and her tender chidings more unmanned me than the chains and handcuffs. In the afternoon she again returned bringing me some of her husband's clothes and a small supply of everything that she thought I should require for the remainder of my route, a couple of shirts, &c. but only being permitted by the gaoler to see them in the open Court I could not assure them how much I felt such uncalled for kindness.

In three days we reached Sarre-libre which was a large depôt for English seamen — several mids and gentlemen were also confined there. Some few who were enjoying the liberty of the Town came to see us on hearing of our arrival, & ordered a supper to be sent to the prison, that they might enjoy passing the evening with us, and before leaving us begged to be allowed in any way to assist us, which we as peremptorily declined, assuring them that we had quite enough to suffice for the remainder of our route: but Mr. Reeding would insist on our taking four *louis* from him, and they gave us some letters of introduction to the Commandant at Bitche. On the second of August we beheld at a distance this dreaded place, at first appearing like old white-washed houses on the summit of a mount in the centre of a valley. As we approached nearer we saw the rampart surrounding it, and the small town of Bitche at its foot. The appearance of the country was wild & inhospitable, and such as to prepare us at once for an awful emigration from our species. About six o'clock in the evening we passed through the Town, and ascended a narrow rugged road leading up to the Fort: its lofty ramparts and heavy gates foreboding little possibility of escape. On entering we were immediately surrounded by a host of our friends, whose overflowing hearts were very much rejoiced at seeing us in such good health after such an undertaking. Indeed it pleased the Lord wonderfully to preserve us through our various peregrinations. They so far succeeded with the Commandant as to keep us that night from the *cachots*, though they could not oppose themselves to our being confined in the *souterrain*, which acted as a kind of panacea to the over-heated constitution of us poor Englishmen. It was so in every sense of the word, being 50 feet under ground, with only a sufficiency of light to see our way, conveyed by a kind of loop-holes from the sides in the top of the arch — if the sun was shining we could just read. We descended by stone steps to this terrific vault large

Mounted *gendarmes* escorting eight prisoners of war who have been
recaptured after escaping. The depot shown is probably Cambrai,
which was established in 1809. From a drawing by Richard Langton.

'A View of the Fortress of Bitche, the Depot of punishment for British Prisoners of War: in the Department of the Moselle and Province of Lorraine.' On the right can be seen two prisoners in chains under escort. O'Brien wrote: 'The high turrets and massive towers of the gloomy fortress stood perched on the summit of a vast rocky eminence, steep and most inaccessible, with a sheer drop of some hundred feet on all sides ... Their very appearance was sufficient to strike the mind with horror.'

enough to contain 500 men — the sides were roughly hewn from the rock with drains of salt water oozing continually, and such a moisture of atmosphere pervaded the whole that in going to bed every night, our sheets were quite humid: but surrounded by our sympathising friends, all thought of our present destined apartment vanished from our mind. The most exciting recitals of our adventures and hearing like hair-breadth escapes drove every murmur to the winds. There is something so cheering in returning to the companionship of your own countrymen after such trials that Butterfield and I were quite led away from all thought of the past but so far as it had prepared us by experience for future undertakings.

The next day we were interrogated by the Commandant as to the cause of our leaving Verdun, which we assured him was no other than an anxious desire to return to our profession and friends from a long confinement which appeared to have no end. He asked where we got our provisions, and by whom we had been assisted in getting out. A citizen in France before giving relief even to a passing mendicant must enquire who he is and demand to see his passport, if he has the least cause to suspect him. We drew up a pitiful story of our sufferings and all we had endured — and had I subsequently been indebted for my escape to any little cheats practised on his sympathy and compassion I should with pain have reconciled them to my mind — and he in his turn made me promises without the least intention of fulfilling them. I entreated him to allow us to be located in a room which my worthy friend O'Brien occupied, with whom I had enjoyed terms of intimacy at Verdun, and with whom I had also served in the *Overyssel*[35] at the commencement of my going into the Navy. We both needed much a little peace and quietness to recruit our strength and spirits, to which the damp air and close confinement of the *souterrain* would not contribute. He said that in about a week if we behaved well we should be changed, but a fortnight expired, and no thought of removing us.

The officers' *souterrain* at Bitche, from a drawing by Richard Langton. Midshipman R. B. James wrote: 'There were about 500 prisoners at Bitche, divided into two Caverns or Souterrains; the largest was for the common sailors; the other for officers and those considered as such . . . The souterrains were very large: 150 feet by 50, fitted up with guard beds on each side, made of strong oak; a straw matrass and a blanket was the bed allowed for two officers . . . We were in darkness all day; from the small windows rays of light would afford us sufficient at times to read by.'

When we had time to look about us Bitche appeared a strange place. A row of large buildings extended the whole length of the fort with an opening in the centre admitting of a communication between front and rear. These buildings occupied the full range of the entire Fort leaving a space of 40 yards in front to the ramparts, and about half that portion in the rear of the buildings. The vaults or *souterrains* were under these buildings and equally extended over the entire range of the Fort, giving great accommodation for troops in time of siege. These *souterrains* were bomb proof. Any of our sailors who had been at all refractory in any of the depôts were sent here and confined to one of these horrid vaults. They were thrown together there without any control over them, & spirits being very cheap nothing could equal the tales that were continually told of them, and their doings, not much to the credit of British Seamen. *Monsr. le Commandant* Clément was continually kept on the alert by them. Their allowance was but a pound of bread and three sous daily, the latter chiefly going to the wine shops.

Butterfield and I had to provide ourselves with a Bed, Bed-clothes, and sheets which were supplied by the shopkeepers in the Town at a very moderate expense. The small *souterrain* to which we were confined was already occupied by about sixty, comprising midshipmen, Captains of Merchantmen, and gentlemen (*détenus*) who had been attempting their escape from other depôts, and like all new scenes had its enlivening charms. We were allowed up at eight o'clock each morning, and by a railing, crossing to the rampart, were prevented on that side from going further, but allowed to go in the other direction round to the front yard, and have free intercourse with the seamen, the door of whose *souterrain* opened into the front yard, and with all others confined to the Fort, many of whom had the privilege of living in rooms in the upper range of buildings. At four o'clock we returned to our *souterrains*, when the *gens d'armes* locked and bolted the doors, counting us all down, and calling over our names. On Fridays and Mondays a member from each mess was allowed to go to the Market to the village. I took advantage of the first morning to go with the party. We descended a zig-zag road, to a very small town, conducted by a few *gens d'armes*. We were kept all together, and went from shop to shop, first to the butcher's then to the baker's &c. again returning to our château, marching in order with our provender in baskets.

Shortly before we arrived at Bitche, an attempt had been made by the prisoners confined to the small *souterrain* in which we were, to escape from a door-way at the bottom of the lower end of the *souterrain*, supposed to be leading through a long passage to a sallying port. A year previous, two Captains of Merchantmen had endeavoured to make their way through this door, but the sentries hearing the noise of their moving along, called the Piquet, who immediately descending, discovered them in the passage, and without remorse sabred them, drawing out their bodies as an example to deter others. Nothing daunted, a large party, determined on again making the trial — having given out that, being the birth-day of our good King[36], great merry-making was anticipated, and wines, spirits, and bread being provided, and also the necessary implements for opening the doors, several of those confined to the upper rooms having learned what was to be the night's undertaking, got permission from the Brigadier of *gendarmerie* to be of the party, expressing a wish to pay due honour to the natal day of George the Third. When the hour for operation commenced, the singing and discordant noise from various instruments increased to a fearful degree. The working party first commenced with picklocks, but that not availing, a lock-saw, the next resource, cut round the lock. It was now found that weighty bolts prevented them from entering. They then determined to undermine the door, and when a little opening was made, a little midshipman was squeezed under, who, with much difficulty, requiring all his strength, forced the weighty bolts to recede, and gladdened all their hearts with the first difficulty being overcome. This was a three-inch-oak-door, but they soon discovered a solid iron one before them in the passage, when again the work of mining was overcome, and our brave little midshipman again footed underneath. He thought that he would have met with the same resistance in shoving back the bolts as before, and gave all his strength to it: but to his surprise it at once ran back at the touch, being set on a spring, and caused such a sound through the empty vacuum that guards and Piquets were instantly on the alert and came down among them, scarcely giving them time to run to their beds. When the Commandant was told that the first door was opened he expressed ridicule, but when he was informed that the iron door was open also, he cursed in the utmost surprise at the English Devils. As all had flown to their beds on the alarm, none were actually caught in the fact: but the *gens d'armes* went to the beds, and those who had cold or dirty feet were conducted off to the *cachots*, and a few days subsequent to our arrival were marched off under a strong guard to Metz, there to be tried for endeavouring to effect their escape. Thus ended this daring and bold attempt — had they reached the anticipated sallying-port their escape would have been complete.

Among the number thus marched off was my worthy school-fellow

Christopher Tuthill, with others of my intimate friends. What would be the result of the trial caused much anxiety among us. In the meantime Butterfield and I greatly recruited our health, and were again planning means of escape, our minds and our eyes alive to every movement. We still wore the appearance of much timidity and dejectedness, and were particularly circumspect in our conversation and our conduct, for we were told that many of the prisoners sold themselves to the Commandant as spies over their countrymen — thus it was difficult to know in whom to confide. My friend O'Brien took us to mess with him. He had some of the sailors for servants, and being enabled to send to market twice a-week, had everything very comfortable at an inconceivably small expense. All kinds of provisions were very cheap. There were constant arrivals of prisoners, who brought us news from the other depôts of their various changes, and many worthy friends effecting their escapes. These arrivals were changing the face of Bitche from its cold damp cells to that of a cool summer's retreat. Letters came from our friends at Metz, telling us that they had been tried before a civil court, and were severally condemned, some to thirteen years at the galley of Toulon, and some as low as seven years. They spoke in the highest terms of the counsel they engaged from Paris to defend them. They were brought to trial under a decree passed in the early part of the Revolution when Austrian prisoners were located in the country, and were constantly deserting, carrying with them intelligence of the nakedness of the land; but says one of these highminded men: 'What intelligence can be conveyed from the *souterrain* of Bitche, and what mother is there here present would not be proud of bearing the son possessing the mind that would dare to undertake effecting an escape from the *souterrains*, over such ramparts, with guards upon guards, piqueted with the extremest diligence?' The Minister of War revoked the sentence, on reading over the minutes of the trial, and all were marched back to the depôt in the same order of chains and handcuffs.

I was daily with the *Maréchal des Logis*, endeavouring to be allowed with my companion to be removed from the *souterrain* to the room which my friend O'Brien occupied, but some excuse was made from day to day — but still assuring me that we should be permitted to remove; at last I got leave to go to the Hospital Room, where I was far more comfortable.

I had been enjoying this change nearly a fortnight, when one day Butterfield came into the room, rubbing his hands, and saying he had leave to move up to O'Brien's room before me, notwithstanding all my exertions to get up before him. Without further explanation, I went to the *Maréchal des Logis*, and implored him so earnestly, assigning my health as the cause of my thus pressing him, and his wife coming into the room at this moment, I entreated her interference and succeeded in obtaining the desired permission. Returning to my friend with a gladdened countenance I found that he had not obtained the desired permission, but it had the effect of urging me on to every exertion.

1 River Kinsin
2 Andalspack River
3 River Iler
4 River Wardach
5 River Lech
6 River Amper
7 River Isar
8 Lake of Kemere

Route of Successful Escape
by Hewson, O'Brien and others
from Bitche on September 15ᵗʰ 1808

THE ADRIATIC

0   25   50   75   100
Scale of miles

V

The Second Escape

I had been daily planning with O'Brien, when we could be retired to ourselves, some way to escape. My friend had a piece of a linen rope long concealed, and was only waiting a companion in whom he could place confidence. The day in which my Hospital Room was vacated by me was that on which our friends returned from Metz. They had undergone much anxiety and fatigue, and having been the messmates with O'Brien previous to their confinement to the *cachots*, we all enjoyed meeting at dinner again, and much happiness ensued — they little suspecting that we were about again to shew that we were nothing daunted by the sentence passed upon them. Several witty allusions were made to our intended escape in very broad terms, but such was the effect of their trial on their nerves that they believed all our allusions were ironical, and when they heard the guns fire announcing our escape, they then saw that we were speaking truth, and regretted that our ambiguity should have prevented them from making to us good offices in strengthening our finances.

As I had already arranged with my friend every requisite for our undertaking, the moment that I could get to his room, and the evening and the night setting in with great severity, it raining, thundering, and lightning the whole night as if sent by Divine Providence to encourage us and embolden our confidence, when our door was locked for the night, on promise of the strictest secrecy, we told our companions in the room our intention, offering to them the same chance and a promise, should the Lord favour our undertaking, not to separate from them till we should cross the Rhine. So many impossibilities and improbabilities arose that only two of our room-mates assented to accompany us. One was Surgn. Barklimore, to whom I had been under many obligations, for his generous and kind attention to me when at Verdun, where I was always in poor health, and which will ever be impressed on my mind. From the certainty which buoyed me up of our succeeding, I almost entirely prevailed on my worthy friend, and the glimmering hope which my sanguine mind gave him sufficed to do the rest. A Mr. Batley, a Dragoon Officer, was the only other person who would be of our party[37].

When we had so far arranged we hesitated not in cutting up our sheets, & preparing all things for descending the dreaded rampart. Our sheets were converted into roping, and joined to that which my friend O'Brien had already in store, and we soon had all in readiness for our departure on our perilous undertaking in which none had previously succeeded. The watch on prisoners was so strict that even a skein of twine could not be conveyed in, much less anything in the shape of a rope, which was the cause of our cutting up our sheets. Before my joining O'Brien he had contrived to get a false Key for the door, and by a friend who had the liberty of the Fort coming to our door under pretence of speaking to us the bolts were shoved back, and all seemed propitious. It was blowing very hard and rain coming down in torrents, and the night set in so dark, that we thought Providence was favouring us, and felt assured of succeeding. We were now alone waiting with palpitating hearts for a sentinel who had been placed at our door, to go into his box: to slip out and away: we had our eye during the whole of the night anxiously fixed on him and observing him with the greatest trepidation: but he was most alert listening & watching every move even under the heaviest rain, and the piquets every ten minutes were making their rounds. When morning dawned we went to our beds with heavy hearts. At eight o'clock the *gens d'armes* came as usual to unlock the door and seeing us all safe took no notice of our door being unbolted: for they had often been in the habit of only locking the door. We had some manoeuvring to keep the secrets of our sheets from the observation of our servants, which we managed by sending them out on some message, when a bed was made that had sheets, and before their return shifting the sheets to an unmade bed. The state of our minds during the day may well be conceived, the more so as we had to endure the succeeding night a disappointment again owing to the alertness of the sentry; for as I before observed there were many spies surrounding us and which made us much fear a discovery. We dare not breathe a word of our intention to any of our friends. We looked from our windows with an anxious eye at the expansive view lying before us of the road (should God prosper our escape) which we should take, passing by Fort Diable similarly situated with Bitche, a protecting fortress on the summit of a mount of about 25 miles south of us which we purposed leaving on our left hand. We were also much amused with the hard thoughts which the old Colonel would entertain of us. In his younger years he had been in the West Indies and lost his arm in an

The courtyard at Bitche: the 'Promenade of the Prisoners'. They were
allowed up from the dungeons for several hours every morning and
afternoon to walk in the yard, which was about 120 yards in length.
The naval officers called it 'being on deck'. The guards and sentries
are well in evidence. Richard Langton made the drawing.

The entrance to the Fortress of Bitche, from a sketch made by Richard Langton, author of *Narrative of Captivity in France from 1809–1814*.

engagement which made him cross, though in the main very goodnatured. At an inspection of the English prisoners under his charge by the general of his District the seamen were drawn up in a line which he admired much: then turning to the *'jeunes aspirants* (Midn.) he enquired how they conducted themselves, saying 'O ma foi — ne m'en parlez pas — quand j'entends qu'un aspirant vient d'arriver, il me frappe aux oreilles, comme un coup de tonnerre — ce sont des jeunes indomptables.' It was certainly very difficult for the old man to keep them from annoying the *gens d'armes*.

As day drew to a close, separating again from our messmates, we felt our hour of trial coming on with a firm mind. We observed the two former nights that the sentries were not so much on the *qui vive* till about nine o'clock, the hour of the night at which we had thought of starting — we therefore determined to try our chance at an earlier hour.

This evening set in very dark — 'twas the 15th. of September [1808] and having again prepared all things, at about seven o'clock we saw the sentry at our door walk to the corner of the building speaking to a friend — at this auspicious moment O'Brien slipped out, throwing himself into the small gutter channel flat on the ground, and was soon out of sight. Committing myself, in a short prayer, to my God's care, I followed, creeping cautiously along, for we had to pass a second sentinel. My friend the Doctor soon came after me, & Batley brought up the rear — thus creeping on all fours we got to a small railing, erected as a division to our yard, giving to each a sufficient time to get forward: & O'Brien having made fast our linen rope to the bars of the railing, cautiously went over the rampart, for much danger was to be apprehended lest the sentinel should at that moment observe us. When I felt the rope slacken I knew that O'Brien was safe. My turn was now come to bid adieu to Castle Misery: with a heart bounding with joy and as light as a feather, over I went, getting down this tremendous rampart hand over hand sailor like. Next came Barklimore, and poor Batley last in the train. When all were safe and we had time to consider our position, we found that we had landed on the roof of a small house supposed to be for a guard. Silence and caution being the order of the day, we jerked on our rope, breaking it as high as we could, and in the off angle from the door sitting myself crosslegs over the roof put the rope round my waist and thus sustained lowered each down. When all were safe, I got down to the edge of the slate and let myself fall, they catching me so as to prevent me hurting myself or spraining my ancles. We now proceeded to the second rampart which was about 40 yards from us, and getting into one of the embrasures, O'Brien fixed a boot hook, which he brought with him, between stones, to which he made fast our rope, and got down the second rampart of 30 Feet, and were equally successful in the third without any alarm*.

About nine o'clock we were clean of all sentinels and off in a run across the fields till we believed ourselves perfectly beyond danger — then halted near a brook to put on our shoes and stockings which we had taken off to enable us to get along in the greater silence. Any one seeing us at this moment would have beheld four individuals almost bereft of reason: in the joy of our hearts we congratulated each other, truly grateful to the Lord for his merciful protection in such a desperate undertaking. Had any of the sentries seen us certain death would have ensued — they have the strictest orders to fire on, or maim any prisoner attempting to escape, and the tales that have been told were very painful. Poor Batley, an officer of Dragoons, who was of our party could hardly believe the reality of his being safe out of such a Fortress, saying that from the moment he assented to accompany us he gave himself over for lost, but would not retrace his steps, lest it might be said that it proceeded from cowardice — but, said he, 'You sailors are Devils.'

Barklimore had not been long in the Fort. He had been engaged in a most arduous endeavour to escape with Captn. [Seacombe] Ellison, [Peter] Kirk, and [Robert] Alison (Purser of an Indiaman) from Verdun. They had not been long on their tramps when they were discovered, and after a short stay at Verdun, were marched to Bitche, and arrived but a short time previous to our escape. There was always something cheering in the arrival of our fellow-sufferers among us, and our warmest sympathy was extended to these dear friends. I could have wished that my late companion, poor Butterfield, could have been with us just now, but it could not have been accomplished. When we had refreshed ourselves at the brook, put on our shoes, and stockings, &c. we offered up to the God of Mercy and Love thanksgiving for such a deliverance. Away then we tramped in full assurance that he would succour us to the end. In the joy and full liberty of our hearts we made a rapid march this night, taking the high road leading to Strasburg, and when day began to appear concealed ourselves in a wood on a sloping hill, at the distance of 25 miles from the château of Tears, and nearly on a line with Fort Diable, a similar fortress to that we had left. This

---

* O'Brien says that the rope broke three times, but on each occasion a long enough piece was left for getting down the next rampart. 'We had let ourselves down by this frail rope a total height of from 180 to 200 feet.'

hasty march was necessary, for guns are fired to forewarn the peasantry of the escape of prisoners to rouse them all to a general search through the country. A considerable reward is offered for the apprehension of prisoners of War, besides confiscation of all they possess about them at the time of capture. The great difficulty we had to contend with in getting over the ramparts precluded the possibility of bringing any provision with us, a flask of brandy and a few pounds of bread excepted. We were therefore obliged to be most provident of our stores — neither Batley, nor friend Barklimore, being able to bring anything. About eleven o'clock our sentinel awoke us to shew us a *gen d'armes* approaching towards us, on the road, underneath our hiding-place. He was riding in great speed, as if to announce our escape to the different ports on the Rhine, and through the country. It caused us much amusement seeing him labouring along for a considerable distance on the road, as if his horse was tiring under him — for we had an admirable view of the country from our position.

I shall long remember the sixteenth of September — the buoyant and elated spirits with which we rose from our hiding-place at a late hour, giving thanks to the Lord for his care and protection of us, and committing ourselves again to him. My friend O'Brien having experienced the treachery of the inhabitants on the roads in this part of the country, we determined to endure every suffering rather than expose ourselves. We went then forward with the utmost precaution, crossing a stubble country which was very fatiguing. We chanced to meet some field-turnips and crab-apples which served for our next day's provision, & happening to pass by two farmer's houses, the dogs forewarned us of our danger. At an early hour we sought a safe retreat in a very close wood. Already Batley began to complain of the fatigue, as he had come away quite unprepared for such an undertaking, having on but a slight pair of shoes which were destroyed by the severe marching though the fields the previous night. Poor Barklimore also felt much weakness, and to keep up their strength my small flask of brandy was occasionally resorted to. The third night we went through a champagne country, our friends limping along in much pain. This had been my friend

Captain Donat Henchy O'Brien (1785–1857) led the successful escape by which Maurice Hewson got out of Bitche and eventually reached Trieste and the Royal Navy. O'Brien was promoted Commander in 1813 and Rear-Admiral in 1852. His book, *My Adventures during the Late War*, was published in several editions.

D.H. O'Brien

O'Brien's third attempt at escape. My friend Barklimore, like myself, had been but once before on the tramp: but Batley was quite new to the fatigues attendant on such an undertaking, considerably increased from the necessities we felt of not approaching the roads, but crossing the country guided by the stars keeping an easterly course for the Rhine. Turnips and cabbage stumps sufficed us for provision.

The Lord blessed me with uncommon health at this time which enabled me to help the *lame ducks*. Towards morning we retreated towards a vineyard, the only shelter we could discover, which afforded us a thick top covering, but underneath, the trestles, which were about breast high, exposed us to a long view. When we had been reposing about an hour we were startled by a gun fired off close to us — the next moment a fox in full speed passed us, but faced round to survey us, and then pursued his course.

Towards noon two gentlemen, apparently in deep conversation, came close to us and halted for some time, talking to each other: but the vines spreading very thick on the trestles concealed us from them. However a third *rencontre* obliged us to seek safer quarters. A woman with a little child which she was leading by the hand in the act of passing, whose little head was under the suspended vines, saw us, and being terrified, roared out, and could not be pulled forward. The mother stooping down under the vines was equally alarmed at seeing four such strange-looking beings lying on the flat of the ground. O'Brien tried to reassure her by saluting her in German, to which she made no reply but hurried away in a great fright. So many alarms caused us at once to change quarters, and in a few minutes we were on the high road, which from its appearance led us to believe that it was leading to some large town. Two women were approaching us from whom we learned that we were three leagues from the Rhine, which was, indeed, most joyful news. As soon as possible we got into shelter in a thick wood that skirted the road, knowing that in the vicinity of the Rhine the *Douanier* guards are particularly on the alert.

A scene from O'Brien's second escape bid in September 1807. He and four companions had been recaptured near Boulogne and were being escorted in chains to Bitche. When close to the fortress the guards provided a waggon and unchained them. One was ill, but the others were allowed to walk. At a sign from O'Brien they made a dash for a nearby wood. One fell in the heavy fallow and was quickly recaptured, but the others reached the trees, pursued by mounted *gendarmes* 'riding in all directions, calling out *Arrêtez, coquins!*' O'Brien made his escape, the others were taken. When he had almost reached the safety of Austria O'Brien was recaptured and taken to Bitche.

At about nine o'clock this night (20th September) we left our hiding place with feelings between hope in the Lord's mercy, and care of us thus far, and our own misgiving hearts: but when I committed myself into His hands, and each of us had embraced as if it were to be our last meeting, on I boldly led. Much difficulty was anticipated in crossing the Rhine. We were led to believe that it was equally arduous with that of getting out of the *fortress of tears*. We were told that *Douaniers* (Custom-House Officers) were stationed at every possible landing place to prevent smuggling — that all people having Boats were required before night-fall to give them in charge to the officers at each piquet, guard-house, where they were chained up. As we approached this noted river we heard horns blowing, as if the guards were challenging each other each half hour. At about eleven o'clock opening out from a wood this famed river burst on our view, & we experienced a joy that few can understand. Though our freedom from the fortress had been but five days, we had gone through much hardship in the time. Like schoolboys we ran to its bank to wash our hands in its stream and drink its water. When we had rested a short time, we followed its course, creeping most cautiously and listening at each step between hope and fear: at last being wearied and fatigued, we set about retiring to look for a place to conceal ourselves for the coming day before light should dawn on us. However I might endure, I felt for my poor companions not having anything to eat since we started, going to concealment for another day without food.

We thought to get to a position where we could observe the movements of the Boats on the water, and after a little reflection, a retreat was commenced: but I took a longing desire to persevere in my search for a Boat a few minutes more, and was in the act of getting through some bushes, when I discovered a small skiff drawn up in a ditch. I ran back for my companions, and no time was lost thinking; and making out paddles out of her bottom boards, and getting her into the river — when behold, four happy fellows on our own element: great precaution was necessary getting out from the shore, lest the sentries should observe us. The night was very calm. Before reaching the opposite shore, as if by Providence, a Scotch Mist set in to conceal us, and unobserved we got in among some flagging when we landed on German ground in safety — thus we overcame this much dreaded difficulty, the Lord being with us.

The mist, with a fog, still continuing, favored our getting into the interior before the people came out to their labour — indeed we were enabled to advance further than we expected. At length with weary limbs, and overcome with every species of fatigue, we stretched ourselves down under shelter of a large tree. Poor Batley was quite exhausted: from the first night of our getting away from Bitche he was taken ill and to keep up his strength I reserved the little brandy I brought with me for him. His shoes were so slight they were no protection to his feet, walking through wet ground; & he was greatly crippled — so much so, that it was in great agony he was able to get on with us.

When the day began a little to advance, and that we were able to rub off some of the mud and dirt from our clothes, making ourselves look wonderfully smart, we ventured on the open road, and went to a small village where we housed ourselves from observation as soon as we could. The good woman of the house set before us all that her larder afforded, which required no sauce to make it palatable. Here we spent some time cleaning ourselves and preparing for the road, and at about eleven o'clock commenced our route towards Rastatt which we learned to be about four leagues from us: so we crossed the Rhine in the neighborhood of Durlach. A good cup of coffee which the hostess provided for us refreshed us greatly and we now set out with renewed strength on our journey, but poor Batley from weakness and sore feet was unable to proceed further. Coming to a small village or rather a retired public-house, we here committed our poor invalid to the care of an old woman, the wife of a shoemaker; it was his own anxious desire to be left on the road — symptoms of fever were appearing, and he could no longer continue the march. The meagre mind of his hostess seemed not much agitated by the passing events: but she appeared quite indifferent as to what country we professed to come from. We led her to believe that we were going to Strasburg, *en congé* [on leave] from our regiment, then in Prussia, and after imparting to our distressed companion all the consolation in our power, and leaving to him a small portion of our funds, we again set forward.

After leaving our companion, we got on such bye-roads, that O'Brien told us we had nothing to fear travelling in the open day: and so much depended on our getting away from the Rhine, that the risk was more than tantamount to the delay occasioned by marching only by night — as in France, we avoided every town. As night approached we came to a large village which we passed through: as it was raining heavily there were no people in the streets: but meeting an old man of decent appearance, O'Brien asked him to conduct us to a lodging-house, where we got comfortably housed for the night — the utmost possible relief to us, particularly as we obtained a room to ourselves, where we sat unnoticed. Though this had

A view of a village in the Black Forest in the early part of the nineteenth century.

been but our sixth day from the mansion of tears, O'Brien and Barklimore seemed greatly fatigued. We ordered supper (being about eight o'clock) and invited the old man to stop with us, but he left us early, and no three weary travellers ever went to beds with a more determined desire for rest: the rain and hail beating against the windows showed us what we should have suffered had we been exposed to its inclemency. The weather on the ensuing morning continued very severe: but after an early breakfast and discharging our bill which was very moderate we took our departure, following the direction of the road, till we met a man and a boy loading a small Donkey-cart whom O'Brien addressed, enquiring the road to Friburg. The poor man left his boy and cart and came with us some distance to put us on the right way. We now kept a southerly course. At Noon we passed the vicinity of the palace of the grand Duke of Baden[38], rather nearer than we could have wished for. In crossing one of the avenues two military officers passed on horseback — for the moment we concealed ourselves but again meeting horsemen in scarlet dresses going at quick pace followed by a carriage with four horses, we turned off towards some huts to avoid them. The people told us that it was the Duke's son. Keeping our road as directed, in the morning we passed through some clean nice villages, which could not but strike travellers particularly coming from France — a degree of comfort seemed to exist reminding us of our own dear country.

Barklimore being a little in the rear was spoken to by a man coming out of one of the houses as if requiring to see his passport — but he followed after us seeming not to understand him. We were much perplexed this evening to arrange as to housing ourselves, — *I* should rather have been inclined to keep the open field, but my companions over-ruled, and with much hesitation we ventured to a house where we found the landlord very drunk and no other person was inclined to notice us: so that through the protecting hand of our Lord we again escaped.

Rising early in the morning, when we discharged our reckoning, we decamped, enquiring our distance from Strasburg, which we found to be five leagues. By ten we were in sight of Offenburg, and made a small circuit across the fields to the left, and again got on our road to Gibenbach [Biberach], and by keeping to all bye-paths and narrow roads avoided observation — at times resting ourselves behind a ditch. At dark we crossed the river Kinzig and proceeded towards Tuttlingen — at midnight halting in a poor small village, but such at that moment as proved a palace to our weary limbs, for Barklimore at this period was very weak from fever and ague. I could not but look on him with much anxiety and as far as my strength enabled me helped him along. We generally got to some room by ourselves so as not to expose ourselves to the inquisitive *passant*, and the Germans were so accustomed to Frenchmen of our appearance, that they seldom shewed the least disposition to pry into our character. In this manner we passed by Baden, Offenburg, and Rothweil, which are large towns that lay in our route, giving each of them wide spaces, and we passed through an angle of the Black Forest, so much spoken of in history, and celebrated for the hordes of robbers which infest it: but though we travelled at day and not by night as in France, it was with excessive precaution — the cold evening damps increasing very much the weak debilitated state of my dear friend — notwithstanding which he never complained. As an instance of his amazing spirits — one evening being about to halt for the night in a house on the borders of the Black Forest, having reason to suspect that we would not be very safe, we determined moving on as quickly as possible to the next town. This was a great disappointment to us, having made a long march this day (nearly 35 miles) and my poor friend only enabled to hobble along by leaning on me. At the hour of about 11, we came to a straggling village in which we housed ourselves very weary, having marched that day more than 40 miles — but while supper was preparing, the Doctor hearing some castanets playing in the kitchen, and some young people waltzing, could not resist the joyful sound, but went down and remained, dancing for two hours.

My friend O'Brien was partially acquainted with this part of the country. In a former attempt to escape he reached as far as Lindau, on the lake of Constance, when he was arrested and reconducted through Tuttlingen on his route to Bitche[39]. While halting in the town many of the principal gentlemen came to see him and expressed high feelings of indignation at seeing two Bavarian Officers reconducting an English Officer who had effected his escape from a French Prison back in chains.

They would have endeavoured his rescue, but the Officers became alarmed and hastened their prisoner out of Town to another stage for the night. Such kind feelings, as well as a promise on their part that if he could effect his escape they would provide him with a passport and a guide to see him in safety beyond the grasp of their common enemy, O'Brien determined now to put to the test, and see what dependence might be placed on them. This town lying on our route, we got to a wood in its neighborhood, and on Sunday morning making himself up as smart as our small packages would allow, O'Brien set out, and with much anxiety as well for poor Barklimore's feeble state as for our general safety, regardless of personal

A nineteenth-century Bavarian landscape.

risk, took the high road leading into the town, leaving us in our retreat. This being the sabbath of our Lord, I trust our minds were thankful to Him for his many blessings and mercies shewn to us thus far.

'Twas a day of great anxiety to us lest anything should happen to poor O'Brien. At last at the close of the evening his well-known whistle told us of his approach; he had gone at once to the Hotel, where he met with a warm reception, and to the astonished landlord told a tale of woe, and a miraculous escape which caused much sympathy: they were for some time closeted in a private room; he told him that when he was given over by the Bavarian Officers to the French Authorities he was treated with every ignominy; from Strasburg he was marched in chains to Bitche; from thence he nobly effected his escape, and was come to put to proof the interest which had been expressed for him on his being conducted through their town a prisoner, shewing his confidence in him by thus coming to his house: but a gloom had now passed over the minds of the Bavarians — they dared no longer shew sympathy to the noble Englishman struggling for the liberties of the world — but with a weak spirit he thought that he could not get him quickly enough out of his house. O'Brien then tried his sordid mind by saying that he had an amber necklace, which he brought with him to give to his wife as a mark of his esteem for the good feeling which she expressed for an Englishman in his distress. This at least seemed to please the vanity of his wife, and with tears in her eyes she overcame the prudent calculations of the cold German, so as to induce him to conceal him at least until she could bring a cutler on whom she could depend to assist him: for though her husband possessed much influence in the town, such a strong French prepossession now existed, that he dare no longer act up to his own desires, and trembled at shewing him the least countenance. The poor cutler had no such qualms: with an honest pride of indignation, he took him under his protection, and at once introduced him among his friends as an old American acquaintance with whom he was engaged on a Pic Nic Party that day, and made him accompany them to the woods. Thus had O'Brien been detained longer than he could have wished; he was accompanied by the intrepid cutler, who, fearless of the passing times, conducted us all to his brother's house, where we were lodged in some garret rooms. Thus was a rest afforded to us, absolutely necessary to our dear friend, who could not longer endure exposure to the evening colds, for fever enfeebled him very much: our kind host supplied all our wants — a warm supper was sent up to us, and beds made comfortable for us.

The following day our noble cutler set his wits to work for us: he called on the Secretary to the Bailiff of the Town, Mr. Smidth, in whom he knew he could confide our secret: this he thought necessary that we might have timely notice to be off should any information be privately conveyed to the police office of our concealment. He tried every means to interest those who had formally made open proffers to O'Brien to shew their sense of esteem for the name of an Englishman — at least he called on them to perform their promises — but they were now lukewarm: the noble-minded German independence dare no longer express itself, and Buonaparte's will was the law of the land, & all were now humbled to the lowest servility. This did not check the exertions of our warm-hearted advocate: as a last resource he procured from Mr. Smidth a passport made up of false materials which we should have been afraid to make use of lest we should have implicated so generous a man.

We remained housed more than a week in our upper story: our poor Doctor was much recruited and in a rapid state of recovery, being able to procure some medicines of which he stood much in need. On Monday morning October the 3rd, accompanied by our faithful cutler, and looking to the Lord as a friend that never faileth those who call upon Him in the hour of need, away we set forward at an early hour on the road leading to Memmingen, intending to proceed to Salzburg, the nearest Austrian Town. We parted from our friend with grateful heart (for such he was to us in need) — he truly deserved our best wishes, not having left a stone unturned to try and serve us, and I cannot but say that he showed a mind and disposition beyond his humble walk; he got us an old German map which was of great use to us. On leaving him we stepped forward with a proud heart looking to our own resources and a confident feel in the protecting hand of our merciful Father that He would in the end bring us to our long-wished-for haven of liberty. We felt greatly refreshed & recruited by our halt at Tuttlingen, and my dear friend the Doctor was quite up in spirits, and the hope of getting over his fever. This day we encountered much difficulty in our march keeping to bye-roads and crossing the streams which checked our onward way. At the river Ablach we very fortunately came to a ferry boat: one of its passengers was a gay-dressed soldier with a large feather out of his cap enough to alarm us: our fortune favored us as usual and we passed over without notice. As the evening approached we got into a house to bring up for the night, but finding a lodger there something too inquisitive, we prudently, under O'Brien's suggestion, again set forward, although we had walked that day more than 30 miles. Our route lay now through a lovely forest, and it was eleven o'clock before we came to a village — which was out of the frying-pan into the fire — for much mirth was going forward caused by a marriage. At length we got housed, but our friend O'Brien being ever on the alert for Police-Officers, and Military Cockades, fancied he observed among those merry-makers some of these woeful countenances, and did not sit quite at his ease: be this as it may, however, their thoughts seemed so much absorbed in the merry scene that we were passed perfectly unnoticed.

At six the following day we pursued our wayward course, looking cautiously at people travelling the road; towards evening we passed the town and castle of Waldsee: the beautiful scenery around us was most striking, and had such an effect on our minds as to cause us to forget for the time our fatigues. The next evening we crossed the Iller, another stream flowing into the River Inn. This brought us into the first Bavarian town. Leaving behind us the territory of Württemberg, circumspection and caution were now particularly called for. The Bavarians were warmly attached to the French interests[40], and would have rejoiced in arresting three helpless British officers back to France: and what added much to our difficulties the poor Doctor was again relapsing into his weak state, for the ague never left him, and the evening dews were very bad for him. Our marching was necessarily protracted, being obliged to walk slower than our usual pace. At our occasional halts at any of the public-houses to procure provisions we reconnoitred very carefully before entering, and if by chance we met with any inquisitive people we always had some ready answer to satisfy their curiosity.

October 8th. we crossed the Wertach, one of the rivers running into the Inn, and directed our route towards Schöngau: and the afternoon turning out very wet, we went early to a little inn in a village, where a shoemaker who was working for the family repaired our shoes, a job much required. The next morning was equally wet but for fear of causing suspicion we moved forward. Towards noon we got under shelter from its inclemency, and dried our wringing wet clothes. The noon of the 11th. brought us to Schöngau, which appeared too large a Town for us to approach, and consequently had much difficulty in crossing the Lech river, till favored by a boat at some distance from the town which was plying a Ferry and made good our anchorage in a small village where we were generally feasted with good fires. Weilheim was the next large town we passed, where we had to cross the river Ammer. These rivers always cost us much delay independent of the great risk to which we were inevitably obliged to expose ourselves. We were now bordering the Tyrolian Mountains, and the scenery was magnificent, but what added much to my spirits at this time, our dear companion the Doctor notwithstanding the inclemency of the weather was infinitely stronger and better than when we left Tuttlingen — the Lord of mercy, giving strong assurance that he would not forsake us, comforted us in all our privation.

Pursuing our course we saw Tölz on the river Amper [Isar], and as our road lay this day over the mountains running nearly on a parallel line with the river, we observed rafts of timber floating down its stream, the river men conducting them in admirable style: this was a new scene to us, and reminded us of our old England. On the 13th. we reached the Inn which flowed majestically below us, as we observed it from the height. We were now near Neubeuern, a large town, but fortunately came to a place where we saw a Boat plying as Ferry, by means of a rope suspended from two poles, on which the traveller was fitted, but which the boat was conducted from side to side. There was a small shed with seats where we found a genteel old man seated awaiting the Boat, which was then at the opposite shore, where the Ferryman was getting his dinner, and would not come for us until one o'clock. We learned from him that we were but fifteen leagues from Salzburg. People in our case are alarmed at every shadow: when one o'clock came we saw the Ferryman accompanied by a grenadier soldier coming to the boat; he wore an immense feather in his hat. We were much troubled to know what to do, but our sweet cherub sitting up aloft soon dispelled our agitation — as the soldier on landing pursued his course not heeding us. On landing on the opposite bank, our joy was very great. We had to change a florin, and the boatman had much difficulty in making out the change. We were but too happy in getting across, and would willingly have left with him the florin, but it might have caused suspicion: however with the assistance of our fellow-traveller he made it out. At about seven o'clock that evening we found accommodation in a small house on the road-side which seemed very private, & afforded us everything we could wish. We were now approaching the last Bavarian Town (Reichenhall) which caused us to enjoy our evening very much, seeing the all-protecting hand of our merciful Father watching over us. The following day we exerted ourselves much to get over the ground, and marched at least twelve leagues, passing a branch of the delightful Lake of Kemese [Chiem], the view of which to sailors longing to resume their much-loved profession raised our spirits. We had but a bad map for a guide, and in consequence made many circuits that might be avoided, if we were at liberty to ask questions, and in a small village off the road made a halt for the night.

146

THE SECOND ESCAPE

We rose early the following morning, and pursued our journey. At eleven we stopped to breakfast at a decent house; it being Sunday morning people were on the road which made us the more ready to halt for a short time; as night approached we got housed, but seeing many inmates around us, under the excuse of our companion the Doctor not being very well, we got to bed early: being now near the confines of Bavaria we required to use double caution: and when we retired we gave full vent to our elated spirits on the prospect of next day's march.

Salzburg: a picture by Quaglio of the Hohensalzburg Castle and part
of the Nonnberg Monastery below.

VI

Arrival in Austria

BEFORE day on the morning of the seventeenth we set off with merry hearts towards Reichenhall. On this day hung all our prospects of succeeding in our perilous undertaking: it set in most lovely, and as we were approaching to a crisis, I fear our thoughts ran too high in looking to our own dexterity and former success in overcoming difficulties. Just as day was breaking we came to a bridge leading into the town, which lay in a valley. At the opposite side of the Bridge lay a small building, which resembled a guard-house, and which caused us some hesitation, but seeing the sentinel speaking to two men, just then going into the town, and a cart coming out, we slipped past unobserved while they were conversing, and turning short round the corner of the house soon got on a road leading in the direction of Salzburg. Believing this to be our last risk, in passing which we anticipated much difficulty, our good fortune naturally caused that mutual flow of thankfulness which can only be conceived by those who have experienced like trials. With light hearts we now talked of the enormous breakfast we would make, the first place we should come to. Passing a small pathway leading across the fields my two companions followed it hoping to shorten the road: but I pressed forward meditating on the great prospect before me of returning again to my dear profession, and my home and all that I held dear in life, when immediately my eye was again struck with the sight of a Bavarian barrier, and arms denoting that we had not yet crossed the boundary. Hesitation in like circumstances is always fatal — I continued on my road and passing the house of the barrier, was questioned by a woman coming up from the river with a can of water on her head, if I had shewed my passport — to which I answered in the affirmative, saying the Officer was sitting in his room smoking his pipe.

On passing over a small bridge I again saw a guardhouse and an officer (hussar) leaning over a railing which fronted it. With an air of *sang-froid* I followed on the road, but he called to me showing that he was not sleeping on his post, and desired to see my passport: but I told him that I only came

149

Salzburg, from a painting by Fischbach, engraved by Sandmann. In the centre rises the Hohensalzburg Castle, built in 1077 and altered in the fifteenth century. To the right are the domes and towers of the Kajetanerkirche, the Cathedral, and the Michaelskirche. Also visible are the Nonnberg Monastery and the River Salzbach.

out from Reichenhall for a morning's walk and did not put my passport into my pocket. My excuse availed nothing — I was desired to return — my embarrassment was great — how to act under my dilemma I knew not — were O'Brien and my dear friend in advance, or in what direction could the pathway have led them — in my uncertainty, I returned to the river — (this appeared neutral ground) and amused myself in throwing pebbles into the water. What could have become of them? As if in a sauntering mood, at length, following the rivulet, I saw the two wished-for friends coming towards me. They followed me to the right, where a wood concealed us from the view of the Hussar Officer. I then told them of my *rencontre*. Their road had led them more in a direct line for the bridge and they escaped the Bavarian Officer's scrutiny. Most inaccessible mountains covered with snow lay in front — there seemed no advance but through a glen which the Austrian guard seemed to watch with the eyes of an Argus: nothing seemed possible but to wade thro' the snow as near the foot of the mountain as we could go. In this manner we made our way nearly two miles when we began to descend by degrees into the glen, believing ourselves past all danger, and we were in the act of getting to the road, when up pops a guard from behind some bushes, and we were immediately surrounded with presented pieces. All talk was vain — the Sergeant with much civility insisted on our returning to his officer, the gentleman to whom I had previously introduced myself. He joked with me on the subject of my morning's walk, and sent for the Bavarian Officer to be present at our examination. As the Officer did not understand English, so neither did we think it prudent to be acquainted with any other language. We made him understand as well as we could that we were Americans and had come from Altona[41], and were going to Trieste to get shipping for our own country again — that we sailed from New York in August in a brig bound to Gothenburg, but having been boarded by an English Frigate in the Channel on putting into Altona, we had been detained by the Danes who under pretence of the crew being English were about making prisoners of us — that they took all our papers from us, and dreading worse treatment we had determined to make our way to Austria, and our desire was to be allowed to get into one of our own ships, at Trieste, for America. The Officer was most courteous and so far as he could understand us, made his report of us. He said that it was his duty to send us over to the Bavarian Officer, but he would send us under an escort to Salzburg to be dealt with by the authorities as they thought proper.

Behold us then once more under bondage; but it was changed to that of Austria from the gritting chains and handcuffs of the French *gens d'armes*.

We were placed under an escort, and marched off for Salzburg — where now was our fine breakfast? and where all the exhilarating thoughts of the morning? The Lord's ways, truly, are not our ways — nevertheless our spirits did not flag — forward we went with our guard, through numberless ambushes of guards — and we saw how fruitless it would have been to attempt to pass the cordon of troops placed between the two states to cut off all intercourse, more particularly on the side of Austria. At every turn round the bushes we saw soldiers concealed — hid in ambush. Our road now led thro' mountain passes in a very wild country. These detached parties that we met so often had even dogs with them lest at night people might try to get over the line. At about four o'clock the great city of Salzburg hove in sight shewing its beautiful spires and domes, the country around looking highly cultivated and improved; surely this must be old England was the first thought in our minds, but the guard of Soldiers around us turned us from our reverie.

Soon entering the city we were conducted to the Police-Office where an elderly gentlemen interrogated us in several languages of which we professed ignorance. When we hailed to be Americans, he turned round much to my amusement to ask the Secretary what language was spoken in America: on being told that it was English, he again turned with a smile and addressed us in really very good English, saying 'Now we can talk together' — and in a friendly good-natured tone commenced his interrogation, taking down first our names. I assumed that of Henderson, as chief mate, my friend Barklimore was Surgeon Manuel, and O'Brien chose to be a passenger named Lincoln. He then dismissed us telling us to bring to him the following day in a kind of written form — our names, parentage, where born, profession, &c. A Policeman was desired to shew us to a Tavern for the night: but the Director desired us in the kindest manner not to leave it without permission. This indeed was an indulgence not anticipated, for our minds were made up once more to endure the horrors of a prison. The Police-Sergeant shewed us a very respectable Tavern, or Hotel, leaving us in perfect freedom. A good supper was our first request. Our mind this day had gone through great changes and anxieties — a new scene was now opening on us and the fact of our having escaped from the hands of the Philistines caused in us fervent thankfulness to our merciful God — our dear Doctor was indeed happy.

We were shewn up stairs to most comfortable beds, and when alone gave vent to the happy change in our minds — a good night's rest completely set us up for further exertions. Awaking early on the morning of the 18th

[October] we felt as if we could stretch out our limbs in perfect freedom: was it possible that we were not under the cruel goading of the *gens d'armes* — could such a thing be possible that we were at liberty? — none but those who experienced a like captivity and sufferings could form an idea of our feelings. We dressed ourselves as well as our tattered garments turned brown would admit, to make our best appearance before the Director at eleven o'clock, with a determination to act with the utmost precaution and circumspection as circumstances would permit.

After breakfast we set forward and as soon as the office opened presented ourselves before the good-natured Director: he wondered that we had no one written document to produce, to testify that we were Americans — we might be telling truth or not — we had no written document to satisfy him — he said that English Officers were frequently effecting their escape from French Prisons, and actually shewed us a book in which many names were inserted, and though his orders were peremptory to send them back to the Bavarian lines, yet 'they always found an Asylum in Austria'. Such an assurance coming from one so high in authority much emboldened us. Our good Father was mercifully watching over us, however. I sat down to draw up my declaration and, when finished, was about handing it to him: but, learning from him that these documents would be sent to Vienna, and remitted to the American Chargé d'affaires and by him communication would be made to the American Consul at Altona, and then if all was true the permission would be granted, and seeing from the candid manner of our interrogator that our scheming would only avail to put off the evil day and that the truth would be unravelled, we came to the resolution, after much hesitation, of confiding our real case to this good old man, who had already much won our confidence. O'Brien then became our spokesman, and when our long captivity and sufferings were made known to him he assured us that 'if he could not serve us he would not injure us'. He wished at the same time that we would leave with him the statement of our assumed country, and continue at the Hotel to be considered as Americans. He promised to use his private influence in our favor with the Minister of Police for our liberation: but he could not look for an answer to his application sooner than 15 days, adding with a smile 'you who have suffered so many years in French prisons may well bear so short a detention *sans ennui* among us Austrians.' He kindly offered to forward a letter to Mr. Concannon[42], a gentleman of some influence at Vienna whom we had known at Verdun, entreating his assistance in our liberation.

Having thus unburthened ourselves, and committed our safety into the keeping of this good old man, we returned to our hotel in much spirits and with light minds and when we had made an early dinner, we walked out to see this fine city in full liberty — no more *gens d'armes*! no more passport! what a happy moment! The large & beautiful cathedral much struck us, and the well-furnished shops — though in reality the town possessed but little to recommend it: yet to us it appeared everything. Before dark we returned to our Hotel, very happy in ourselves. Having much idle time on our hands, we applied our minds to learn German and from close application were making great proficiency in it: we endeavoured to chat to every one who had patience to bear with us. The great victories of Sir Arthur Wellesley[43] were in every one's mouth — his letters detailing the battles were in every paper, and caused general exultation — the Austrians bore the most heartfelt love and pride in speaking of our beloved country. These victories were the first obtained over Buonaparte's generals, and consequently caused great rejoicing: we grieved much that we were denied the privilege of acknowledging ourselves.

We daily walked about looking at the Citadel and the Town, and the ramparts — looking out for a place whence we might effect our escape in time of need. The town was surrounded by hills on all sides, affording but a limited view of the country; and being treated by the Director with such confidence we would do nothing to cause suspicion and kept literally to the town: but our minds were so elated with our present liberty, that every passing scene was the source of much enjoyment to us — and seeing my dear friend the Doctor fully recovering his health & spirits was cause for much thankfulness — he was our best German scholar, and was all life and spirit.

On the 11th. morning of our arrival at Salzburg a Police Officer from the Director came to our room: we were all lounging in our beds engaged in much cheerful conversation: his appearance startled us: he told us that he was sent by the Director to request that one of us would go to him as soon as possible. We were much puzzled to know what he wanted — could we be saying or doing anything to cause annoyance? However, *poor pilgarlic*[44] was deputed, and I made great haste to his office, and was soon in his presence — when, great indeed was my surprise, to find that he had a communication from the Minister of War, to give us our passports to Trieste, and that we might go there when we pleased. Nothing could be more kind than his manner in seeing me so overcome by his good news, and he expressed everything that a good man could only experience in being the medium of procuring for me and my companions such a boon. He

A drawing by Cassas, dated about 1800, of the town and port of Trieste, seen from the St Theresa Mole. On the hill behind the town stand the old castle and St Just's Cathedral.

apologised to me for the poverty of his bureau not enabling him to do more than discharge our expenses at the Hotel, saying, 'this is not I assure you what my heart would dictate to British Officers'. Returning to my companions I was much affected in framing some little tale of my interview not to awaken too suddenly their feeling, or rather I must truly acknowledge to play on them. The Hotel was at some distance: at one moment so overcome was I that I would commence running, and then recollecting myself would stand still to collect my feelings: at last, coming in to the room, I put on myself a sorry countenance, and premising with a species of growl and ill-humour at everything we had been doing, grumbled something about an order having come, and the sooner we got our breakfast the better. 'My God!' exclaimed poor Barklimore: and my friend O'Brien was about turning in his bed in much despair: but when I told them of the glad tidings which I had to communicate, they made but one bound into the middle of the floor, and joy was truly shed on our countenances: my friends were soon dressed, and at breakfast.

Our first duty was to go in a body and offer thanks to the benevolent worthy Director for the kind part he took: and the old man glowed with delight on the expressions of our gratitude. He was not alone satisfied with making his official report of us as Americans, but exerted his private influence for us under our real characters, and awakened their sympathy in our cause: as our finances were very low, he made our passports to be prepared for us as foot-travellers, and we were told that they would be ready for us in half an hour.

When we returned to the Hotel we found a letter awaiting us from Mr. Concannon, saying that the Court of Austria was most favorable to Englishmen, and that there was no hesitation in giving us passports: but what was most acceptable he sent an order to his Banker to give us credit for any money we should want: thus then the Lord had filled up the measure of our wants: and feeling we could now travel *en diligence*, we settled to have our passports changed in accordance, and took our places to start at four o'clock. This was most fortunate to our poor invalid — for his ague had never left him. We again returned to our benevolent Director who was much gratified at hearing that our finances were renewed. All things settled, behold then three happy individuals *en route* by the Diligence, accompanied by one morose old man not at all suited to harmonise with the buoyancy of our spirits at this moment. Our minds were too much occupied with the happy change in our situations to heed much the uneasiness of our unwieldy conveyance. Could it be possible that we were returning to our dear friends after such a confinement, & undergoing such hardships? Truly God is full of mercy and love to such as call upon Him faithfully. Our profession was now open to us, and we could look forward to advancement as others had done. The shaking of the Diligence would again rouse me from my reverie — it was rough travelling for my dear friend, but he partook equally of the delight of our minds. We passed over precipices and through passes in the mountain road that at another moment would have required much nerve to go through — at times our drivers would call to us to alight in the heavy snows, travelling on the edge of precipices when the least stumble of a horse would have thrown us headlong over. At the fourth stage we were all changed to a covered waggon which jolted us sadly. We were also much annoyed by six noisy boys going to school — they naturally were turning us in their merry-making into much ridicule, but the young rogues only came as far as Villach with us, at which place we arrived at nine o'clock on the following morning. Our passports *bien entendu* were demanded, but we were now *tout en règle*, and no longer under fear of the *bureaux*.

Thence we proceeded to Klagenfurt, a large beautiful town which attracted much our attention. On presenting our passports at the office we discovered that the Diligence had carried us some miles out of the road marked out by the Director at Salzburg, but they were very civil in the police office, and made no hesitation in setting our passports right. At the Hotel at which we halted for the night, we found that our next day's route would lead us over a very steep mountain, and on enquiring at the Post-house we found they would require a double lay of horses for posting, and we were told that by walking we should get over much earlier. Early in the morning as soon as we could see our way we set forward: we had eighteen miles of ascent, and as many to descend on the opposite side: there were post-houses at convenient distances, where we occasionally halted and refreshed ourselves. At seven in the evening we reached a village at its foot, where our passports were revised, where we refreshed ourselves. We recommenced our route *en carosse* for Laubach, travelling all night, and at break of day entered the town. Our *voiturier* drove us at once to a very comfortable and superior kind of an Hotel: and we were not long tumbling into the arms of Morpheus, in most comfortable beds. At about 9 o'clock on the morning of the 31st of October we went to the police office about our passports, and in passing through the town we could not but admire the clean streets, and well-dressed females. 'Twas market-day and the young ladies were all out with maids following them, having neat market-baskets

A more embracing view of Trieste and its harbour. In the foreground
can be seen the lighthouse at the end of St Theresa Mole.

under their arms — we could not but admire their fair beauty, so much superior to any we had been accustomed to look at in France — they were making their marketing and saluting each other in a familiar affectionate tone. When all was arranged at the office and we had made a good breakfast we again set forward, much elated at drawing near to Trieste.

I cannot but relate a singular *rencontre* we had on the previous night — going up a lonely steep mountain as much to warm ourselves as to lighten the load on our one horse cabriolet, we all got out and commenced walking up the hill — O'Brien a little in advance, and the Doctor in full chat with me. We heard O'Brien speaking Irish to a man on the road — and on coming up we found several soldiers surrounding him. It turned out that a guard of twelve men were stationed here to preserve passengers from being robbed on these lonesome roads and on seeing O'Brien they challenged him, and coming into conversation, not being able to speak German, he asked if any of them spoke French or Italian: but being answered in the negative, he inquired if any spoke Irish, on which there was an immediate rush out from the guard-room and all mouths were opened at once. These poor soldiers had expatriated from Ireland shortly after the rebellion in that country in 1798[45] and were permitted to enter into the Prussian Service. Two Battalions at the time were taken out of the Prisons, and transmitted to Prussia, but at the time that Prussia was obliged to submit to the yoke of Buonaparte[46], these Battalions were sent to Austria, and thus employed. Nothing could equal the boisterous joy of these poor creatures in meeting in us brothers from their fatherland: their canteens were immediately brought out from the guard-room, and when they were told that we were prisoners effecting our escape from French prisons, they rushed in for their muskets, and swore that they would accompany us to see us safe out of the country, and even accompany us to old Ireland. We had much ado to disentangle ourselves from these warm-hearted poor men, leaving with them some little trifle in remembrance of our passing visit.

In this manner did we proceed till approaching the heights immediately over Trieste from town to town which was indeed to us travelling with much interest: but I cannot pass over our excitement in seeing, on ascending a hill, the expanse of the Adriatic as now lying before us — the Town of Trieste underneath us — its Mole containing the Russian Squadron[47], and a frigate under sail in the offing, which our Driver told us was an English Frigate. We had each suffered every humiliation & severity of treatment that it was possible to inflict on individuals whom fortune of war placed in their power, and whose very misfortune claimed protection.

The generals over the prisoners at the several depôts, being subject to no control over them, swayed an unlimited authority of severity, and oppression, and by base acts of low cunning extorted from the poor prisoners as much of their small subsistence as was consistent with prudence — for the most trifling irregularities — and worked on the weaknesses of the more wealthy for larger exactions to their cupidity. Our hearts were at this moment truly lifted up to the Lord in earnest thankfulness for his unseen care of us in such an escape from their clutches, and felt much sympathy for our many deserving friends, yet under their merciless Jurisdiction.

We now were all eagerness to arrive, and soon getting over the ground enquired for the police office. The Director received us very kindly and told us that his relative the Director of Salzburg had written to him mentioning our sad story. He seemed to feel a kindred interest in us and our escape, but wished us still to assume the American tale. He directed us to a noted Hotel where everything was served in the first style of splendor. When we got possession of our rooms, and had settled to dine at the Table d'hôte, we sallied forth to visit the American Consul by the wish of the Director. He received us with great civility, and directed us to Mr. Donalon, formally Vice-Consul for England and still doing (though not officially) all the business. He received us most cordially and told us that H.B.M. Ships *Unité* and *Amphion* were cruising off the port, and when the Boreas[48] then blowing ceased he would prepare a boat for us to carry us to the nearest in shore of them.

We returned to our Hotel in very good spirits, and sat down soon after at a long table laid out with every delicacy of the season and a large assemblage of merchants, & gentlemen from various quarters of the globe, each taking their allotted places at the table. We chose our station next the staff of Russian Officers who always got in a group at the head of the table. *Le dîner prêt* was soon announced and *Messieurs les Américains* playing a judicial part on the good things set before them — now and then by some quaint remark telling the Russian Officers who we were. Our conversation with each other was at first confined to French — but a stern seriousness seemed marked on their countenances, and we shifted our conversation to Italian, relating several anecdotes of Russian Midshipmen when in our service; on something that I was saying, O'Brien remarked that I would let the 'cat out of the bag,' at which one of my neighbours could not retain a half smile. The dinner being removed, O'Brien retired with me to our room to write to our dear friends at Bitche, being the first moment we felt ourselves at liberty to address them lest we might be traced through the Post-office — but we now through the kind Providence of our Lord felt perfectly safe. We had been absent from the room for some time, but on our return found our friend the Doctor seated in the midst of the Russian officers apparently very happy among them. On resuming our seats they intermingled with us, and called for some champagne wine, and general unanimity was drunk. When we had passed a social evening, they invited us to seats in their private boxes at the Opera, and before allowing us to part, introduced us to their lodgings where supper was prepared for us in superior style — great conviviality ensued, and all parties retired much pleased with the evening, and we with the hospitality shewn us. One of the Officers kindly accompanied us to shew us the way to our Hotel — we obliged him to come in; and some rum punch being called for, friend O'Brien said he observed our guest to have smiled when he remarked that I was letting the 'cat out of the bag', which convinced him that he could speak English, and that we should leave off our foreign *lingo*, and speak under true colours. Our friend acquiesced at once, and a very pleasant hour was passed before our companion took his leave for the night.

The following day on our way to see Mr. Donalon, we put our letters in the Post-office. I directed mine in German to my poor friend Tuthill and as it was all written in Italian, it was handed to him without any observation. At the appointed time (ten o'clock) we saw Mr. Donalon at his house — he introduced us to Mrs. Donalon, an Italian lady of great beauty, and two very sweet daughters, who much resembled her. Mr. D. gave us Ten Pounds, on our draft, and told us that a Boat should be in readiness for us as soon as the Borea ceased. On leaving Mr. Donalon poor Barklimore returned to the Hotel being still weak, but O'Brien accompanied me to the heights outside the town to refresh ourselves in looking at the broad ocean, and feasting our eyes on the sight of a small British Frigate proudly standing in, daily reconnoitering a large Russian Squadron moored in the Mole, and capturing vessels hourly, in their view, even under their guns — 'twas truly flattering that we belonged to a country and service that swayed so triumphantly — feared and admired by all Europe.

The frigate HMS *Unité* (40 guns), from a drawing by Robert Mercer
Wilson, who served on board her in the Mediterranean from 1805 to
1808. The *Unité* and *Amphion* were cruising off Trieste when
Hewson and O'Brien reached the end of their successful escape run.

Rear-Admiral Sir Alexander Ball (1757–1809), by an unknown artist. Nelson, who called his friend 'the polite man', ordered him to blockade Malta after it had been seized by the French in June 1798, when Bonaparte was on his way to Egypt. From 1802 until his death Ball was Governor of Malta; he was a wise man, immensely popular, and idolized by the people of the island.

VII

The Voyage Home

ON Monday afternoon the weather became more moderate, and our anxious hearts were all alive to the hope of getting afloat. We were early with Mr. Donalon who kindly engaged the boat for us. He did not think it prudent for us to embark till after dark — but at the appointed time, eight o'clock, how great was our joy at getting afloat. We were hailed by the guard vessel *en passant*, and the boatmen went through the ceremony of shewing our pass, and then away we went without further interruption. Well might we say with the Psalmist 'Cast thy burthen on the Lord, and he will sustain thee.'[49] We now stood out, in the direction in which we hoped to meet a Frigate, which we had seen in the offing in the dusk of the evening, but not finding her, we rowed in under Capo d'Istria to await the morning. Before day we weighed our grapnel, and were about to proceed in the same direction, when we observed a boat pulling towards us which proved to be one from the *Amphion*, commanded by Captain Hoste[50]. At first we concealed ourselves imagining that it might have been a Russian Man-of-War boat sent after us — how great then was our joy to find ourselves under a British Flag. Lieutenant [George Mathew] Jones the officer in command permitted us to remove to his boat, saying that he could not take us off to his ship till about noon — we therefore discharged the one we brought with us from Trieste, paying him nearly Ten Pounds for bringing us off. We wrote a few lines in pencil to Mr. Donalon telling him of our being once more on our own element, and that we had paid the boatmen Eighty Guilders. O'Brien soon recognised in Lieutenant Jones an old shipmate (he having formerly served on board the *Amphion*) — their happiness at meeting under such circumstances may be conceived.

Our route to the *Amphion* (which stood down towards Fiume during the night) lay along shore. Lieutenant Jones boarded several Austrian vessels bound to Trieste, not worth detaining, actuated by a liberal mind, not wishing to bring misery on poor helpless individuals. In pulling along we rounded Capo d'Istria, and opened a bay in which we saw two vessels, near

165

one another, becalmed, the largest of which showed Venetian Colours[51], and fired a shot at us — the immediate animation which glowed in our little crew, only fourteen in number, deserved a better fate — our small bow-swivel[52] was fired in return — we struck our masts and sails and all prepared for action — such was the exciting spirit, shewing the indomitable courage of British seamen — it was a proud moment for us who had been so long absent from such scenes.

It being calm, we were soon alongside the largest of the two: but unfortunately we pulled between them and thus were exposed to the full fire of both vessels, who poured on us a shower of musketry, and some musketoons. Just as we were laying our boat alongside two of our small crew were killed and three were wounded. Every endeavour was made to board — but they made such a determined defence that we were obliged to retreat and our only trophy was bringing away some brass musketoons, which they flung on our heads when they had fired them. Lieutenant Jones, my friend O'Brien, and three men were severely wounded — the Pilot, and two men were killed. Lieutenant Jones desired me to take the command and get the boat off as soon as I could. There being at this moment some confusion after shoving off I had to place the men at their oars: but one poor man was shot, when in the act of taking the oar from me: consequently I was obliged myself to pull the oar. When I got to a little distance from them, we put our boat in trim and proceeded to join the *Amphion* which we soon saw at a considerable distance in the offing.

It seemed as if our buoyant presumption in believing ourselves beyond the reach of fate was to meet its due reprimand — our escape from capture was only effected by the individual exertions of our small crew. We afterwards learned that these were privateers — the one which we attempted to board had sixty men. Her captain and four men were killed in our struggle — we were exposed to the musketry of both vessels from going between them. On approaching near the *Amphion* I made the signal of distress, and the barge was sent to our assistance, and took us in tow. When we reached the ship a slung chain was let down for the wounded. I did not wish to leave the boat till all the poor wounded were hoisted up — and on

Captain Sir William Hoste (1780–1828) from a portrait by W. Greathatch. He served under Nelson in many actions, notably at St Vincent, Santa Cruz and the Nile.
A Norfolk clergyman's son, like Nelson, Hoste thought of the great Admiral as a 'second father'. He was created a Baronet in 1814.

making my appearance on deck, Captain Hoste believing me to be the Captain of the vessel (from my foreign appearance and dress) which had caused such a painful scene, addressed me in French in a very angry tone — he was much excited at seeing his brave officer, and so many of his poor men killed and wounded — but when I told him that I could speak English he became still more angry — but when he could coolly listen to my story, nothing could equal his affectionate reception of me — it was at once the most generous and liberal, each officer vying with each other in supplying me and my companions with whatever we wanted in clothing and linen, and one of the officers was kind enough to give up his cabin to O'Brien. On his wound being examined it was found that a Musketoon ball had passed through the flesh of his right arm — and though but slight, Surgeon Moffat wished to lay it open, which operation the poor fellow bore with the greatest composure. The wound of Mr. Jones was more serious, and prevented him from resuming his duty for some time. When misfortunes and trials cease, how soon does buoyancy possess the mind, and all sufferings become buried in oblivion!

Some vessels were observed from the mast-head of the *Amphion* (which had now anchored) going from Venice to Trieste by an outlet or river, running parallel with the shore, but separated from the high sea by a lofty shingle embankment. Mr. Bennett the first Lieutenant was ordered in the barge accompanied by the gig to examine them, and though I had but got afloat the previous day, I begged to be allowed to accompany him as interpreter. The gig being a light boat soon distanced the barge, and the young midshipman in command, when he reached the beach, left his boat taking his crew with him, and ran across the strand which separated him from the river disappearing from our sight. Mr. Bennett was much agitated at this thoughless conduct, and when he reached the beach, he sent me with a Marine to see after his young scion and his crew, and took the gig in tow to bring her round to where the creek or river had its outlet, which was nearly two miles from where I landed. When left with the Marine I crossed the strand, and seeing several vessels coming towards me from the direction of Venice, and several fishing-boats plying about, I made one of them come to me, and take me and my fellow-marine off to a xebec[53] just passing: she proved to be laden with hemp and cordage. I made the fishing-boat assist in towing her, for the winds were very light. We soon overtook another vessel laden with wine, which I obliged to throw a rope into me, and got some more boats ahead to tow us. We next came up with a timber vessel, which I also took in tow, and lastly came up with my young hero, the object of my search, in a vessel laden with wine, which being sweet tempted him and his crew to make free with: thus my charge became most irksome — Mr. Bennett not in sight — and having now more than sixty people surrounding me, including the crew of the four vessels and the boats which I made to tow us: however, no way daunted, I kept my marine with his musket in the bow and remained watching at the tiller myself, and my musket ready for any emergency. With the light breeze and the assistance of the boats ahead we were getting down pretty smartly — passing one small village a musket shot was fired at us. We also passed a large vessel laden with timber, which had stranded, and then much to my joy the Barge with Mr. Bennett hove in sight. He was soon alongside, and praised me for my determined and prudent conduct. When we got out of the river we proceeded to the *Amphion*. I had promised to the crews that I would intercede with Captain Hoste for them that they should be liberated, which was most humanely granted.

Nothing could exceed the kindness and attention of Captain Hoste — a plate was always placed at his dinner table for me. He took great interest in the incidents of our escape, and hardly allowed me to leave him a moment. At length an opportunity offered of sending us to Malta, in the *Spider* [14 guns]. Captain Hoste made us most generous offers of money to equip ourselves at Malta, and at least made me accept a Letter of Credit on his agent residing there, lest I should find difficulty in getting bills cashed. He also gave me a letter of introduction to Sir Alexander Ball, the governor of Malta[54]. My friend O'Brien under the care of Dr. Moffat was again restored to himself, but still kept his arm in a sling.

Our passage in the *Spider* was tedious: off Corfu we made a capture of a sloop proceeding to that island and on the 8th. of December arrived at Malta: but in consequence of our communication with the Prize we were put under quarantine which prevented our waiting on Sir A. Ball. We therefore wrote a joint letter to him stating our case and soliciting his introduction of us to the Commander-in-chief, as also an order for a passage to England for Mr. Barklimore. He most kindly ordered us to be received on board H.M. Frigate *Proserpine*, then sailing out of the harbour to join Lord Collingwood off Toulon, telling us that from Captain Hoste's kind mention of us, he had written to his Lordship in strong terms of us. The merciful hand of the Lord shewed itself now — the Quarantine officer would not give us *pratique*[55] till a few hours after the *Proserpine* had sailed off, for she was captured on her arrival off Toulon: when we should again have been plunged into prison *malgré nous*.

To our great joy the *Amphion* arrived, and much to our surprise our poor forlorn companion Batley came passenger in her, the poor fellow whom we left so desolate in the mountains of Baden. His debility was of short duration. He got the old woman with whom we left him to procure a pair of shoes for him, when he again set forward on his road. In following the direction I had pointed out to him before separating, which would lead him to the Danube, he got entangled in a wood, and believing himself engulphed in an endless forest, he became quite frantic, calling for me, and calling for O'Brien, fancying that wolves would devour him, running about in various directions; but in one of his races he got out of the wood, and was soon after stopped by some *gens d'armes*, who confined him in a small *cachot* in a miserable village, where he was locked up in a room under the guardianship of an old woman, who gave him his food in through a small latch-door: but on no account could he induce the old creature to open the main door, and allow him to breathe a little fresh air in this miserable place. They took his clothes from him, leaving him in perfect nudity. Not seeing a hope of overcoming the persevering caution of the old beldame he commenced picking at the old wall of the room, and soon brought out a stone, and by persevering made a hole of sufficient space to get out: but having no clothes he could not proceed and only thought to surrender himself to the next authorities: and proceeding with this intent, he enquired at the first village at which he arrived for the Mayor's house, and on relating his tale to him, ending with saying that thinking that he could not be worse off, he had come to give himself up to him. The Mayor, being a kind-hearted man, brought him down some of his old clothes, and adding three *louis* said he would not be instrumental in detaining a poor Englishman a prisoner, and told him never to say that he had been near his residence, and mentioned to him that an English lady lived at no great distance, and told him to go to her for some aid.

The following day he made out her château, and had the mortification to be denied the most humble relief. Away then he faced for the Danube, trusting to the small relief obtained the previous night, and by dint of perseverance obtained sight of the long-wished-for river. He hovered on its banks till seeing a boat laden with coal passing, he was fortunate enough to get a passage in her to Vienna, to which place she was bound. No sooner was he immersed in the coal than he got so black and dirty and looked so like a beggarman, that no questions were asked him by the police as he passed along. Thus he reached Vienna much about the time we were leaving Salzburg, and having made out Mr. Concannon for whom I had told him to make enquiries, and to make use of my name in introducing himself. When presenting himself at his door, he asked if he was the person whom Mr. Hewson mentioned in a letter lately received, and being assured that he had escaped out of Bitche with him, Mr. Concannon generously took him into his house, got him some clothes, and kept him some little time to recruit from his fatigues, and then obtained a passport for him to enable him to proceed to Malta. Here he remained for some little time, and being a good billiard-player, lived by his ways and means, till an opportunity offered for his going to England, and from thence I heard that he went to India and there rejoined his regiment.

When relieved from quarantine we were received most kindly by Sir Alexander and Lady Ball, whose sympathies for us were of the warmest kind. Sir Alexander taking me into his private room made to me the same generous offer of pecuniary aid as Captain Hoste, and nothing could equal the interest he took in all about us, and ordered us a passage in H.M. Ship *Leonidas* [36 guns]: he even in a letter to Captain Hope[56] requested that his tailors might be employed to make clothes for us. After an affectionate parting with my dear friend Barklimore, whom Sir Alexander kindly provided with a passage to England, we proceeded to Minorca where we arrived on the 18th., and were sent to the [*Royal*] *Sovereign* [100 guns], Admiral Thornbrough[57], who ordered us a passage in the *Kingfisher* [16 guns] to follow the *Ocean* [98 guns] to Gibraltar, where it was supposed Lord Collingwood had proceeded, having parted from the Fleet in a heavy gale of wind from the Eastward, off Toulon.

When off Malaga we learned from the *Weazle* that his Lordship, meeting a strong westerly gale, had borne up for Malta. Captain Tritton consequently returned to Minorca, and was a second time despatched to Malta, where we arrived on the 24th. of January, and learned to our unspeakable joy that the *Ocean* was undergoing repairs at the Dock yard. I cannot here but pay a just tribute to a dear departed friend Captain [Charles] Coote, then first lieutenant of the *Ocean*, who the moment that he learned that I was in the *Kingfisher* came to see me — the full impression of my long and severe sufferings rushing forcibly on his affectionate and warm-hearted mind we mutually found relief in tears — we had commenced our young naval career together under Admiral Oliver[58] and, though for many years separated, it had not closed the forces of friendship. The following day we were removed to the *Ocean*. The officers received us with a deference not usual on such occasions, and our wonderful escape from the hands of the Philistines caused us everywhere to be looked on with much sympathy —

the officers taking great interest in the relation of our adventures, collecting in groups wherever we were to be seen — from Lord Collingwood to the lowest class of officer, all seemed to vie in attentions.

Sir Alexander Ball, not content alone in having written in our favour to Lord Collingwood, now came on board and in person interceded for our promotion, nor would he leave his Lordship's cabin till assured that we should get the first vacancy on his Lordship's list.

When the *Ocean* had completed her repairs, the Admiral sailed for Palermo, where the Court of Naples had removed, when Murat over-ran the country[59]. They were most assiduous in their attentions to Lord Collingwood — large parties were hourly visiting the ship and O'Brien and I were kept in constant motion shewing the live lions about the Ship.

From Palermo we sailed for the Fleet off Toulon; Lord Collingwood put our patience for some time to the test — as he afterwards said in a letter to the Admiralty that he might in person judge our ability to commit to us the important charge of commissioned officers. On the first of April [1809] my friend O'Brien was provided with a vacancy in the *Warrior* [74 guns] and on the 11th. his Lordship gave me an order to act as Lieutenant in the *Magnificent* [74 guns]. During my stay on board the *Ocean* my worthy and dear friend Coote never ceased in his kind attentions to me, and on my appointment would insist on giving me money to supply myself with uniforms and necessaries required on my promotion. We parted immediately from the fleet for Malta, whither the *Warrior* had proceeded a few days previous. At our approaching the island it blew a very heavy gale of wind on shore, which to strangers was awful: and Captain [George] Eyre and Mr. Randall, the master, being perfect strangers to the place called on me to take the command of the ship: but as we approached the entrance the sea was so heavy that they both became very nervous, and I found it necessary to exert some firmness by taking the helm myself: but when I rounded the rock and ran her up into smooth water, they shewed very altered countenances — had the Captain or master at such a critical moment interfered, it might have been attended with very serious consequences.

Above: Valetta: the Grand Harbour from the upper part.

Below: Valetta: the Grand Harbour looking inwards.

The Letter in which Midshipman Maurice Hewson was appointed to act as Lieutenant of HMS *Magnificent* instead of Lieutenant Downer promoted. It was signed off Minorca on 11 April 1809 by the Rt Hon Cuthbert Lord Collingwood, Vice-Admiral of the Red and Commander in Chief 'of His Majesty's Ships and Vessels employed and to be employed in the Mediterranean.'

This letter from Lieutenant Maurice Hewson to their Lordships at the Admiralty in London is dated Malta 21 April 1809 and encloses a letter from Vice-Admiral Lord Collingwood directing him to act as Lieutenant in HMS *Magnificent*.

My friend O'Brien and I again enjoyed mutual happiness in meeting, and during the time our ships were repairing were as much together as our respective duties would permit. We called on Sir Alexander Ball to express to him our deep sense of gratitude for the position we then held. His reception of us was that of a kind father, divested of all ceremony, and seeking what more he could do for us, as he considered that our promotion to Lieutenancies was no remuneration for our loss of time in prison. He desired us each to write a narrative of our sufferings and escape, during our cruise and that he would forward them to the Admiralty with the view of following up our promotion. We were invited to his state dinners and were introduced by Lady Ball to all his friends, and the Captains: indeed, nothing but the kindest hearts could dictate such attentions. To our unspeakable joy a party of our Bitche friends who had effected their escape from that fortress about this time, arrived at Malta — a Mr. [George Hall] Dacre, whom I had well known, Captain Ellison, and Mr Kirk — their sufferings had been no less severe than those we had undergone.

As soon as our refit was complete, we sailed from Malta for the Adriatic where we were employed blockading Corfu. During my vacant moments I was occupied writing this unvarnished tale of facts to hand to Sir Alexander Ball: but melancholy to relate it pleased the Lord to remove him from this pilgrimage of pain and sorrow, just as we returned to Malta: and O'Brien and I had the sad grief to be chief mourners at the funeral[60]. The whole island seemed to mourn this good and estimable man, who not only bore the highest palm for distinguished merit in his professional career in the Navy (he commanded a ship in the Battle of the Nile[61] for which he was knighted) — but his urbanity and even-handed justice gained for him as

Above: This painting by Powell shows a British 'third rate' (64–80 guns) entering Port Mahon, Minorca.

Below: HMS *Magnificent* clawing out from the lee shore in the Basque Roads off La Rochelle and the Ile d'Aix, on 17 December 1812. While at anchor she was driven by a gale among a group of islands. Only the superb seamanship, leadership and presence of mind of her captain, John Hayes, saved the ship and the 550 men on board. This was the ship of the line to which Maurice Hewson was appointed as Lieutenant in 1809. He served in *Magnificent* until the summer of 1812, and had left her before the incident shown in this aquatint by J. F. Gilbert.

176

An aquatint of Gibraltar, dated 1808, by H. A. Barker and J. B. Harraden. Henry Aston Barker (1774–1856) painted many panoramas between 1802 and 1822, including Malta, Venice and Constantinople.

Samuel Taylor Coleridge in 1814. This portrait by Washington Allston (1779–1843) was painted eight years after Coleridge returned from Naples and Rome. Before that he had worked for ten months as private secretary to the Governor of Malta, Rear-Admiral Sir Alexander Ball. In 1809 he started a philosophical and theological periodical, *The Friend*, which lasted for nine months; and in this he wrote in praise of Ball, whom he admired profoundly both as a human being and as a public figure.

Allston was an American painter of seascapes, portraits, landscapes, mythological and Biblical subjects. He graduated from Harvard University in 1801 and visited London and Paris in the following year, returning to Boston in 1808. This portrait of Coleridge — who admired Allston's work — was painted during a second visit to London. Allston returned home for good in 1818.

Governor of Malta the love and esteem of its inhabitants. For an account of the singular graces and excellences of Sir A. Ball's character, see those essays of Coleridge called 'The Friend'[62] — of which it is said, there are few better specimens of genuine English Prose, employed to do honour to a genuine English character.

Through the generous interference of Admiral Oliver with whom I had sailed in the early part of my servitude, my acting order as Lieutenant was confirmed by the Admiralty.

Notes

1   The passage from Virgil's *The Aeneid*, Book I, runs:

> ... multum ille et terris iactatus et alto
> Vi superam, saevae memorem Iunonis ob iram,
> multa quoque et bello passus, dum conderet urbem
> inferretque deos Latio; genus unde Latinum
> Albonique patres atque altae moenia Romae.

In his translation, published in 1951, C. Day Lewis rendered this as follows:

> ... a man much travailed on sea and land
> By the powers above, because of the brooding anger of Juno,
> Suffering much in war until he could found a city
> And march his gods into Latinum, whence rose the Latin race,
> The royal line of Alba and the high walls of Rome.

2   See the Introduction.

3   Cuthbert, first Baron Collingwood (1750–1810) assumed command after Nelson's death at Trafalgar, and spent the next five years in the Mediterranean, cruising off Sicily and Spain and blockading Toulon. He died at sea on 7 March 1810, on board *Ville de Paris*, while sailing to England in the hope of recovering his health.

4   In 1803 a plot was hatched to remove Bonaparte as First Consul. This royalist plan was fostered by *émigrés* in England, several British politicians, and Admiralty officials. Georges Cadoudal and his followers were landed in France by the Royal Navy, meetings were arranged with Generals Pichegru and Moreau, and a double agent revealed the plot to Fouché and Bonaparte. Moreau, though he mocked various Consular institutions in public, declined to be actively involved. In February 1804 he and the others were arrested. Cadoudal was guillotined, Pichegru was found strangled in his cell, but Moreau, the victor of Hohenlinden, though sentenced to two years in prison, was banished by Napoleon and went to America. The First Consul believed that the Bourbon Comte d'Artois, living in England, was implicated, but he did not appear. Perhaps acting on misinformation, Napoleon

had the young and innocent Duc d'Enghien kidnapped in Baden and brought to Vincennes, where he was given a summary trial, then shot — to general outrage in Europe.

5　William Pitt (1759–1806) served as Prime Minister from 1783 till he resigned in 1801, and again during 1806 until his death.

6　*Procès-verbal*: an interrogation and the taking down of particulars.

7　This soup was made from pulses such as beans, peas and lentils.

8　*Bucentaure* (80 guns) was to be Admiral Villeneuve's flagship at the battle of Trafalgar.

9　'Troublesome fellows', 'awkward customers'.

10　Bridewell was the 'house of correction' in London.

11　Napoleon's first plan had been to transport his invasion army across the Channel in merchant vessels and his guns on flat-bottomed boats, but there were too few of the former, so in September 1803 it was decided that the army too would embark on *bâteaux plats*. In the words of Lieutenant-General Sir Henry Bunbury: 'Through the summer and autumn of 1803 every river and port from Ushant to the Texel was ringing with the clink of hammers and the din of multitudes employed in building the greatest flotilla that ever darkened the sea.' Despite every effort by the Royal Navy, during 1804 over 1,700 were assembled in Boulogne and nearby harbours.

12　The word 'cartel' meant an agreement between two states at war for the exchange of prisoners. Numerous attempts to negotiate such a general exchange broke down or were quickly dishonoured.

13　A 'depôt' was a place of confinement for prisoners of war.

14　The recently launched 36-gun *Shannon* of 881 tons was in fact wrecked on 10 December 1803, off Cape La Hougue, south of Barfleur.

15　Captain Edward Leveson-Gower, who reached Verdun as a prisoner in January 1804, was released on 25 May 1806, and returned to England.

16　Jahleel Brenton (1770–1844), born on Rhode Island, served in the American War of Independence and in the Swedish navy before he became a lieutenant in the Royal Navy in 1790. Within ten years he had reached the rank of Post Captain. While commanding the frigate *Minerve* he and his crew, including his Lieutenant, John Fennell, and his Surgeon, Alexander Allen, were captured when the frigate ran aground near the entrance to Cherbourg harbour. While under fire for ten hours from French batteries eleven of his men were killed and sixteen wounded. After three years spent as a prisoner of war, Brenton was exchanged for a French Captain taken at

Trafalgar and he went to England. He later served in the Mediterranean, and was created a Baronet in 1812. Promotion to Vice-Admiral came eventually in 1840.

17 Louis Wirion (1764–1810), born at Logny in the Ardennes, was the son of a pork dealer. After obtaining his discharge as a dragoon in 1786, he studied law, but the French Revolution swept him back into the army as an officer. He fought at the battles of Valmy and Neerwinden and at the siege of Namur. Promoted to *Général de Brigade* in June 1794, Wirion commanded the *gendarmerie* of the Army of the Sambre and Meuse. By the end of 1801 he was *Inspecteur Général de Gendarmerie*, and two years later, on 3 December 1803, he was appointed Commandant of the town and citadel of Verdun, with responsibility for all the British prisoners of war and *détenus* there.

   The British, while none too flattering about Madame Wirion, a former washerwoman, described the General as a contemptible tyrant whose rapacity knew no bounds and who abused his position to extort huge sums in indulgences granted from those whom he knew to be rich. Bribery, the sale of passports, and taxes levied on every club at Verdun were complemented by a series of fraudulent measures which in the end led to his ruin. When his scandalous activities were discovered by his masters in Paris, the Emperor set up a commission of enquiry in March 1810, but on the day it was due to submit its report, Wirion blew out his brains in the Bois de Boulogne.

18 The Irish Legion was raised in France in November 1803 from Robert Emmett's United Irishmen who had fled after the suppression of the 1798 rebellion. For the next two years Napoleon sent agents secretly to Ireland to recruit and ship men to France. Later the Irish Legion became the *3e Régiment* of foreign troops in French service.

19 *Hussar*, of which O'Brien was Master's Mate, was wrecked near Ushant (now the Ile d'Ouessant) off the tip of Brittany on 8 February 1804. The ship's company, less her Captain, made Brest harbour by superb seamanship in fishing-boats and surrendered to French warships there.

20 This debtors' prison, pulled down in 1844–6, used to stand between Ludgate Hill and Farringdon Street in London.

21 Tuthill and Robert Thorley were, respectively, Midshipman and Master's Mate in *Impétueux*. Thorley, promoted to Lieutenant while at Verdun, eventually escaped in 1813.

22 *Traiteur*: the keeper of an eating-house.

23 The Patriotic Fund was founded in July 1803 by the subscribers to Lloyd's

of London 'to animate the efforts of our defenders by sea and land' by providing a fund for the relief of themselves when wounded or taken prisoner, and of their widows and orphans. By August 1809 a total of £425,000 had been received and over £330,000 expended.

24 Tuthill, with O'Brien, a fellow Midshipman named Henry Ashworth, and a Sub-Lieutenant, John Essel, escaped on 29 August 1807. They headed for the Channel rather than towards the Rhine, but were apprehended at Etaples and brought back to Verdun in October.

25 William Gorden was serving as tutor to young Mr Storer from Jamaica when they were both arrested. Storer escaped on horseback after tricking a gullible guard, but Gorden remained in Verdun until 1814. He became chairman of the fund for dispensing funds for the relief of poor prisoners.

26 Sarrelibre was pre-Revolutionary Sarrelouis. The name was altered so as to eradicate any reminder of King Louis XVI.

27 In August 1805 Austria joined Britain and Russia in the Third Coalition against France, whereupon Napoleon took the army he had assembled at Boulogne for the projected invasion of England and marched it to the Danube. On 20 October he defeated the Austrian forces under General Mack at the battle of Ulm. He entered Vienna and then, on 2 December, inflicted a crushing defeat on the armies of Russia and Austria at Austerlitz.

28 General Oudinot (1767–1847) was not created a Marshal until July 1809. He commanded 10,000 *Grenadiers de la réserve*, who left the Boulogne camp on 16 August 1805, and entered Germany via Strasburg.

29 The first visit could have been on 26 September 1806, when he was on his way with the Empress Joséphine to conduct the campaign which led to the defeat of Prussia on 14 October at the battle of Jena-Auerstädt. Napoleon stopped for breakfast in Mars-la-Tour, between Verdun and Metz.

30 The Treaties of Tilsit were signed on 7–9 July, 1807, by the Tsar Alexander and by Napoleon, after a private meeting on a raft moored in the middle of the River Niemen. Present at Tilsit was Marshal Joachim Murat (1767–1815), who became King of Naples in the following year. The Mameluke referred to was Roustam, who had been presented to Bonaparte in Cairo in 1799 and who thereafter served Napoleon as personal bodyguard until 1814. On his way back from Tilsit Napoleon passed through Königsberg, Dresden, Frankfurt, Mainz and Bar-le-Duc, reaching Paris on 27 July. To visit Verdun meant a slight detour.

The Mamelukes, who originally came from the Caucasus to Egypt as slaves, were ruling the country in the late eighteenth century. Under Murad Bey and Ibrahim Bey they offered strong resistance to Bonaparte's conquest of Egypt, but were defeated on 21 July, 1798 at the battle of the Pyramids. It was his admiration of their martial qualities that induced Bonaparte to take one of the Mamelukes for his personal bodyguard.

31   Mr Kitchen, probably aged about sixteen, was on his way to join the Honourable East India Company's service as a writer, or clerk.

32   Midshipman Butterfield, from HMS *Impétueux*, had arrived in Verdun the previous May. He was later to make a successful escape from Bitche.

33   The Côte d'Or is the region of vineyards stretching south-west of Dijon and embracing such famous names as Beaune, Gevrey-Chambertin, Nuits-St-Georges, Pommard, Volney and Meursault.

34   Narva lies on the southern shores of the Gulf of Finland, about 100 miles west of Leningrad.

35   In 1796–7 Hewson had served in HMS *Overyssel* (64 guns), a captured Dutch warship, in the Downs, latterly as a Midshipman. See Introduction.

36   King George III was born on 4 June 1738.

37   Little is know of Batley, who was destined for service under the East India Company. But Dr Archibald Barklimore had been captured by a large French privateer off the coast of Ireland in August 1802, while returning from the West Indies. A fellow prisoner, Seacombe Ellison, described him thus: 'He was of a cheerful, jocose disposition, and had a talent for learning the language, and imitating the manners of the French. He had all their grimaces, their every motion; in fact, he was to all outward appearance a genuine Frenchman.' After the wars he became a reputed surgeon in Charlotte Street, Bloomsbury.

38   Karl Friedrich, Grand Duke of Baden, joined the Confederation of the Rhine under Napoleon's protection in 1806. He was succeeded in 1811 by his son Karl Ludwig Friedrich.

39   After his unsuccessful escape attempt from Verdun in August 1807 (*see* note 24), O'Brien was determined not to go to Bitche and he managed to escape while being escorted there. He alone made his getaway and he almost reached the safety of Austria in November, despite knowing no German, but after a daring run for his money was stopped outside Lindau and asked for his passport. He was arrested and the inevitable sentence was to be taken back to prison — to Bitche.

40   Bavaria had been made into a kingdom in 1805 by Napoleon, and was an original member of the Confederation of the Rhine, remaining a firm ally of the French until 1813.

41   Altona, on the Elbe, was then at the western outskirts of Hamburg.

42 Mr Lucius Concannon had been a *détenu* at Verdun, where he was chief organizer of theatricals, using his house as greenroom, wardrobe and rehearsal room combined. The proceeds were given to local charities. He and his wife once gave a fête for 120 people to celebrate the Prince of Wales's birthday. In 1806 the Concannons were given a passport allowing them to travel to Vienna.

43 Wellesley, afterwards Duke of Wellington, defeated the French in Portugal at the battles of Roliça and Vimeiro on 16 and 18 August 1808. Strictly speaking they were not the first victories over Napoleon's generals, since the battle of Maida on 6 July 1806 saw the defeat of General Reynier's troops in Calabria by a British force under Sir John Stuart.

44 'Pilgarlic' is a disparaging term for 'poor creature'. Here it refers to Hewson himself.

45 The Rebellion during the first half of 1798 was largely confined to Wexford, and the rebels were defeated at New Ross and Vinegar Hill. A French landing arrived too late to give any support, and the troops involved were beaten on 8 September by a British force under Lord Cornwallis.

46 Prussia became subject to Napoleon after her defeat in October 1806 at Jena/Auerstädt and the French entry into Berlin.

47 The Treaty of Tilsit had obliged the Tsar to leave the Third Coalition. One result was that Vice-Admiral Seniavin, Russian Commander-in-Chief in the Mediterranean, withdrew his squadron from the Adriatic, but he left some unseaworthy ships — three ships of the line, a frigate and three sloops — under Commodore Grieg. These were taken to Trieste and lay inactive there for several years, watched by the Royal Navy which was prepared to destroy the Russian ships rather than let them fall into French hands.

48 The Boreas is the north wind.

49 Psalm 55, verse 22: 'Cast they burden upon the Lord and He shall sustain thee; He shall never suffer the righteous to be moved.'

50 William Hoste (1780–1828) was a protégé of Nelson. With *Amphion* and other ships he captured or destroyed over two hundred French or Venetian vessels in 1808–10, and destroyed a further forty-six sail in 1810. On 13 March 1811, Hoste with four frigates defeated a Franco-Venetian squadron of eleven ships off Lissa. He was created a Baronet in 1814.

51 By the Treaty of Pressburg in December 1805, after Austerlitz, Austria ceded Venice and other territory to Napoleon's new Kingdom of Italy. In 1808 the Venetian navy under French control comprised three frigates.

52 A small gun mounted in the bow and moved on a swivel.

188

53 A xebec was a small, three-masted ship, lateen-rigged and often with some square sails. It was used in the Mediterranean as a warship — the Austrian navy included four xebecs — and also by corsairs.

54 Alexander Ball (1757–1809) entered the navy as a result of reading Defoe's *Robinson Crusoe*. In 1798 his perseverance in towing Nelson's *Vanguard* when she had lost some of her masts in a gale led to a warm friendship between the two men. Nelson, who called Ball 'the polite man', ordered him to blockade Malta which had been seized by the French when Bonaparte was on his way to Egypt. In 1802 Ball accepted the post of Governor of Malta and was promoted Rear-Admiral three years later. Nelson told a friend that the Maltese adored Ball, and he wrote to Emma Hamilton: 'He is a great man, and on many occasions appears to forget he was a seaman. He is bit with the dignity of the Corps diplomatique.'

55 *Avoir libre pratique* means 'to be out of quarantine'. Here the word means 'clearance'.

56 Later Admiral Sir Henry Hope (1787–1863). He commanded cruisers in the Mediterranean between 1808 and 1812.

57 Admiral Sir Edward Thornbrough (1754–1834) first went to sea with his father in 1761. During his early career he was wounded, shipwrecked and publicly commended. He later took part in the battle of 'The Glorious First of June', 1794. He was promoted to Admiral in 1813.

58 Robert Dudley Oliver (1766–1850) towed the prizes from Trafalgar in 1805. He served in the American War of 1813–14. Hewson had served with Oliver on convoy duty to Quebec in 1798 when Oliver was Captain in *Nemesis*, and had been under his command again in *Mermaid* in the Mediterranean, watching Toulon in particular. See Introduction.

59 In 1806 Napoleon ousted King Ferdinand IV and the Bourbon dynasty from the mainland portion of the Kingdom of the Two Sicilies, created the Kingdom of Naples, appointed his brother Joseph to be the sovereign, and sent Marshal Massena — Hewson is wrong in saying it was Murat — to enforce the new policy and to subjugate the region. When Joseph became King of Spain in 1808 it was Murat who took his place in Naples.

60 Ball died in October 1809.

61 He commanded HMS *Alexander* at the battle of the Nile on 1 August 1798.

62 Samuel Taylor Coleridge (1772–1834), who served Ball as private secretary on Malta from July 1804 until the following year, described Sir Alexander as 'a very extraordinary man — indeed a great man. And he really is the abstract Idea of the wise and good Governor.' In his series of essays entitled

The Friend Coleridge praised Ball as 'the best and greatest public character that I have ever had the opportunity of making myself acquainted with.'

Coleridge, known for poems like 'The Ancient Mariner', 'Kubla Khan', 'Christabel' and 'France, an Ode', also wrote very fine prose, including *Biographia Literaria*. Opium ruined his health and his poetic creation, but until 1818 he remained an outstanding critic and lecturer. He was also one of the most fascinating conversationalists of his day.

Bibliography

Alger, John G., *Napoleon's British Visitors and Captives, 1801–15* (London, 1904)

Boys, Captain Edward, RN, *Narrative of a Captivity, Escape and Adventure in France and Flanders during the War* (London, 1817, enlarged ed. 1864)

Brett-James, Anthony, *General Graham, Lord Lynedoch, 1748–1843* (London, 1959)

Coleridge, Samuel Taylor, *The Friend*, 3rd ed. (London, 1837)

Ellison, Seacombe, *Prison Scenes* (London, 1838)

Fraser, Edward, *Napoleon the Gaoler* (1914)

James, William, *Naval History of Great Britain, 1793–1820*, 6 vols. (London, 1822–24)

Langton, Richard, *Narrative of Captivity in France from 1809 to 1814* (London, 1836)

Lawrence, Henry, *Picture of Verdun from the Portfolio of a Détenu*, 2 vols. (London, 1810)

Lewis, Michael, *The History of the British Navy* (London, 1957), *Napoleon and his British Captives* (London, 1962), *Social History of the Navy, 1793–1815* (London, 1960)

O'Brien, Donat Henchy, *My Adventures in the Late War* (London, 1814), (enlarged ed. in 2 vols. 1839; new ed. by Charles Oman, 1902; originally pub. in *The Naval Chronicle*, vols 28 to 31)

Oman, Carola, *Nelson* (London, 1947)

Pivka, Otto von, *Navies of the Napoleonic Era* (Newton Abbot, 1980)

Raikes, Rev. Henry, *Memoir of Vice-Admiral Sir Jahleel Brenton, KCB* (London, 1846)

Warner, Oliver, *A Portrait of Lord Nelson* (London, 1958)

Acknowledgements

The editor and publishers would like to thank the following for their help in the research for this book: Miss Rosemary ffolliott; Commander G. Hare RN (retd); Captain David Hewson; Mr John Hunt; the Staff of the Library at the Royal Military Academy, Sandhurst.

The publishers are grateful to the following for their kind permission to reproduce copyright illustrations: Bibliothèque de la Musée de l'Armée, Paris (Photo Hubert Josse): 47, 48; Bibliothèque Nationale, Paris: 8/9, 38 (above), 44/5, 52/3, 64/5, 67 (above), 74, 75, 76, 79, 86, 98/9, 102, 108/9, 111 (above, below); The British Library, London: 23; British Museum, London: (John Freeman Group) 142, (Eileen Tweedy) 138/9; Hôtel de Ville, Verdun: 58; Lloyd's of London: 68, 69, 70; Musée de la Marine, Palais de Chaillot, Paris: 37 (below), 163; Museo Civico di Storia ed Arte, Trieste: 159; National Army Museum, London: 41, 73; The National Maritime Museum, London: 17, 32/3, 37 (above), 38 (below), 62 (below), 104/5, 167, 177 (above, below), 178/9, (Eileen Tweedy) 156; National Portrait Gallery, London: 180; Public Record Office, London: 15, 55, 174, 175; Victoria and Albert Museum, London (Eileen Tweedy): 112, 148, 150/151.

The passage from the translation of *The Aeneid* by C. Day Lewis, published by the Hogarth Press, is reprinted by permission of A D Peters & Co Ltd.